T0208015

RESPONSE
THEOLOGY

Agape Love Powered by Holy Spirit

John T. James, PhD

WESTBOW
PRESS®
A DIVISION OF THOMAS NELSON
& ZONDERVAN

WestBow Press books may be ordered through booksellers or by contacting:

WestBow Press
A Division of Thomas Nelson & Zondervan
1663 Liberty Drive
Bloomington, IN 47403
www.westbowpress.com
844-714-3454

ISBN: 978-1-6642-7488-4 (sc)
ISBN: 978-1-6642-7489-1 (hc)
ISBN: 978-1-6642-7487-7 (e)

Library of Congress Control Number: 2022914492

Print information available on the last page.

WestBow Press rev. date: 08/29/2022

Sometimes, I retell biblical stories citing scriptural references, but when no specific biblical reference is used, I will not cite the editions I read to retell the story. For example, I retell as a shortened version of the Good Samaritan story from Luke and Jesus's encounter with a Samaritan woman at the well from the gospel of John.

About the Cover

The Hubble Space Telescope picture is from the central region of the Whirlpool Galaxy. Scientists see the dark center as an 'X.' Christians see a dark cross within the image that reminds them that they must dedicate their lives to following Christ who died on a cross that they may be indwelled by Holy Spirit.

I acknowledge the role of my daughter Laura in selection of this image. For Christmas 2005 she gave me her painting of this image. It has been part of my heart and mind since then.

This book is dedicated to Alex, my firstborn son who had his life stolen that I might find the Way.

> Jesus said: I am the Way; I am Truth and Life. No one can come to the Father except through me.
>
> —John 14:6 NJB

The author's proceeds will be given to Servants in Faith and Technology, Lineville, AL.

CONTENTS

ACKNOWLEDGMENTS

I wish to thank friends who patiently gave feedback as I wrote each chapter of this book. They know who they are: Harry, Tony, Ryan, Cameron, Amanda, Mimi, and Gretchen.

PROLOGUE

By profession, I am a medical scientist having retired from NASA several years ago. Traditional Christian doctrines once created conflicts in me as I tried to believe what I was taught as truth, but I kept running up against what I knew to be true as a scientist. I was troubled by inconsistencies in what I was expected to believe.

My scientific interests spanned many disciplines—astronomy, physics, chemistry, pathology, and finally toxicology. This book is intended to revitalize Christian thinking by combining reason (science) and a fresh look at the Bible. I am not a theologian, which gives me the freedom to reject unreasonable doctrine, but at times, that may open the door to theological challenges from those experts who bore into the crevices. I hope to keep my thinking at top level—seeking overall messages of truth rather than microscopic examinations of selected biblical passages.

As a scientist, I bear witness to the elegance of the Creator's will. As a Christian mystic, I understand that there is a realm of truth that science cannot fathom. As a former atheist, I had to ask myself, *What God is it that I do not believe in?* For atheist readers, I offer a fresh idea of God in which you may find truth and experience.

As a scientist, I have witnessed phenomena of nature that you cannot dream of understanding, nor can I. As a radio astronomy student at the University of Virginia in the late 1960s, I was at the vanguard of the study of pulsars—newly discovered stars that rotate so rapidly that their "beam" can be observed up to thirty times per second.[1] I was able to do this with what was then the largest moveable radio telescope in the world (300 feet across) in Green Bank, West Virginia. The pulsar that produces such rapid pulses is embedded in the crab nebula (fig. 1), which was born when that star exploded in 1084 CE. Astronomers call such violent explosions supernovae. Interestingly, this was thirty years after the great schism (separation) between the Roman Catholic Church and the Eastern Orthodox Church.

Figure 1. Crab nebula imaged by the
Hubble Space Telescope (NASA)

---

[1] S. J. Goldstein Jr. and J. T. James, "Accurate dispersions for thirteen pulsars," *The Astrophysical Journal* (1969) 158: L179–82, http://adsabs.harvard.edu/full/1969ApJ...158L.179G.

As a pathology graduate student working at the National Cancer Institute in the late 1970s, I was involved with a team of leading cancer researchers. My task was to discover the molecular basis for the differences in susceptibility to a carcinogen that causes colon cancer in some strains of mice but not in other strains. I found that the persistence of specific types of damage to DNA (deoxyribonucleic acid) in the colons of the mice was directly correlated with the causation of cancer.

During my research, I marveled at the wisdom with which DNA was created to order the basis of all higher life on this planet. Only four bases organized in different patterns form long, double-stranded sequences of DNA; these aggregate in pairs to form our genes. And these gene sequences can be repaired by molecular mechanisms that continuously sustain the integrity of DNA unless it is attacked by an overwhelming army of carcinogen molecules. Under persistent attack, the cell's DNA is thrown into chaos that does nothing more than cause uncontrolled growth of cells. This is cancer. I could observe these invasive cells with a quality light microscope and tumors with my naked eye (fig. 2).[2] But in the strain of mice capable of repairing the damaged DNA, no tumors were developed, and only a few precancerous cells could be detected by microscopy.

---

[2] J. T. James, A. M. Shamsuddin, and B. F. Trump, "A comparative study of the normal histochemical and proliferative properties of the large intestine in ICR/Ha and C57Bl/Ha mice," *Virchows Arch (Cell Pathol)* 41:133–44 (1982): https://www.ncbi.nlm.nih.gov/pubmed/6134379.

Figure 2. Tumors produced in the colons of white mice by a chemical carcinogen. Black mice given the same dose could repair the DNA (molecular) lesion that was mutagenic and caused cancer. Tumors (bright lumps) are evident when colons are resected lengthwise as shown.

My scientific efforts have taken me to be on the Space Shuttle only a couple of hours before launch grabbing samples of the vehicle's atmosphere for analysis in the toxicology laboratory at Johnson Space Center. I concluded that it took more guts than I possessed to ride one of these machines into space.

More recently, I have had the privilege of being given enough authentic moon dust to lead a team of remarkable scientists who completed a study of the toxic properties of this exotic gray dust.[3] My hope is that one day, our findings will guide engineers who build habitats to sustain humankind's permanent presence on the lunar surface.

My early journey as the son of Christian parents involved trials at several churches in the small city of Garden City, Kansas. I have a now treasured RSV Bible presented to me in 1954 by the First Methodist Church. Once my family moved to Wichita, Kansas, we participated in a Presbyterian church that was being formed.

---

[3] C. W. Lam et al., "Toxicity of lunar dust assessed in inhalation-exposed rats," Inhal Toxicol. 25(12): 661–78 (2013), https://www.ncbi.nlm.nih.gov/pubmed/24102467.

I grew up in that church being subjected to Sunday school and painfully sitting through sermons. I seldom had conflicts with my loving mother, but when it came time for me to graduate high school, the church asked all the graduates to wear their caps and gowns to the church service. I was vehemently opposed to that because I did not think pomp belonged in church. Looking back, I am ashamed of my behavior. My mom was denied the joy of seeing her firstborn honored in church as a high school graduate.

One other religious experience outside this Presbyterian church involved a lovely girl I was dating. She, a Baptist, convinced me to attend a revival. Being smitten, I would have done anything to preserve our relationship. I showed up for the revival one Sunday evening and sat clueless next to her. I endured the revivalist's dynamic exhortation to follow Jesus, and then the call was made for anyone who had not been saved to raise a hand. Foolishly, I did. The revival's salvation team descended upon me like starved locusts as everyone in the congregation prayed for my salvation. I would not have it. I remained officially unsaved, and I lost the relationship I valued with this girl.

As a young adult, I drifted with my circumstances. In college at the University of Kansas, I vividly recall sermons by a preacher who left listeners highly unsettled about how they were living. He was extremely popular among students. While I was in the army, I attended a few Catholic services.

I fell in love in the mid-1970s with the woman I would ultimately marry, and we attended a Presbyterian church in the Washington, DC, area. Our specific purpose was to get to know the minister who would marry us. Except for the church not being air-conditioned and thus hot as Hades during our August wedding, that worked out fine. My faith journey had been a tapestry of pieces that did not fit because I never examined my beliefs seriously. Except for remaining officially unsaved, I went with the flow.

My religious journey was anemic and convoluted until 1977, when my wife and I discovered a wonderful, small Methodist church in the countryside not far from us in Severn, Maryland. It was there that we shared the joys of rearing two young children and the simple thoughts that went with believing what we were told by church preaching.

When we moved to Houston in 1989, we quickly found a large, warm church formed in the early days of human spaceflight in Clear Lake, a Houston suburb. Again, we bought into the faith traditions that Methodists were supposed to believe. I taught Sunday school and led Bible studies. Youth mission trips to poor areas taught me to appreciate the vast difference between my worldly blessings and those of poor Christians. Given my highly limited construction skills, I did my best to be a blessing to less fortunate folks. Our family was completed with a son born in 1991. In 2000, my wife and I parted with our older son, Alex, so he could study computer science at a university. He came home with a lot of questions about Christianity that I could not intelligently address.

In the spring of 2002, Alex attended the air force's ROTC summer camp in South Dakota. It was his first time far from his family. He was lonely and challenged by learning leadership responsibilities and maximizing the physical fitness requirements.

With only a few weeks remaining in camp, he wrote a journal entry about his little sister's graduation and birthday. I'll share it so you know him a little.

> We had our second physical fitness test today, and I improved 45 points from a 427 to a 472. I am going to go for it—500 points—on the next test. I'm not going to get the base liberty this Sunday. I already missed my sister's high school graduation, and now I'm not going to get to call her on her 18th birthday, which happens to be Sunday. Oh well, service before self, even though family has nothing to do with self. High school graduations and 18th birthdays occur only once in a lifetime, and it really [disappoints me] that I am going to miss it. I have decided that this Air Force separation is not for me. I want to have a family and settle down in one place for a while, but oh well—I feel as though I owe my country some service, and that is what I am going to give them ... Tomorrow is Sunday and I am going to try to go to church to hopefully gather some inner peace and lower my stress level ... I am somewhat concerned about my calves; they have been painful for the last couple of days, and they don't seem to be getting any better.

I remember well the day he returned home, and I saw him walking toward us on the airport ramp. He walked like a man possessed of military bearing. He was going to make a fine air force officer.

In the fall of 2004, my entire religious framework experienced an earthquake measuring 9 on the Richter scale. The foundations of my faith were destroyed when my twenty-two-year-old son died. He had collapsed while running but self-recovered, and he was evaluated for five days in two hospitals. He called home a few days after discharge from the hospitals to report that he had been given a clean bill of health. I thanked God for his apparent good health. That belief was shattered three weeks later when he collapsed again while running, but that time, he remained in a deep coma until he died three days later.[4] In those three days, hundreds from our church prayed for his life and scores drove from Clear Lake to be with us during our vigil that ended in his death in College Station.

I have fragmented memories of the three days during which he was dying. I remember his little sister nearly fainting when she first saw him comatose with all sorts of tubes coming out of his face. I remember my call to my parents in Kansas telling them that one of their grandsons was in a deep coma after collapsing while running. The whole family gathered to be with us. I remember asking about my son's blood enzymes and being shown levels that were the hallmark of massive tissue destruction. I remember praying on my knees beside his bed, "Not my will but God's will be done." I remember having to sign a DNR (do not resuscitate) paper when the doctors started shocking his heart to get it restarted. When he died, the four of us in his immediate family gathered at his bedside, held each other, and cried and cried and cried. I remember having to tell those gathered in the waiting room that my son had died. That evening, the lead pastor at our home church conducted a service for us in the hospital chapel. I

---

[4] J. T. James, *A Sea of Broken Hearts*, Author House, 2007 https://www. authorhouse.com/bookstore/bookdetail.aspx?bookid=SKU-000234829.

remember my stoic father crying beside me during the service. I was numb with grief.

Once my son was buried, I began to vent my anger toward God, the omnipotent God in whom I was taught to believe. For about three weeks, I seethed with bitter anger toward God. If God were truly omnipotent and had just let my son die or caused his death, I had no use for such a god. Indeed, I had prayed that God's will be done. Then as the storm clouds of my grief began to lift, I started to understand that God had been there all along working through those folks who had come to love on my family during our time of deepest suffering. They had responded to our suffering. No one wants to be where someone's child is dying. No one. But they came anyway. And they stayed until he died.

It was only in the wake of the loss of my son that I began to take a scientist's view of what I had been taught to believe. Was Christianity a cruel hoax to mollify the masses including me? Would another religion be better for me? I even read the Qur'an as best I could. How far could reasoning take me in my belief journey, and how much did I have to rely on faith? As I formed a rational belief, I found that it was seriously tested.

As a board-certified toxicologist with a PhD in pathology, I was troubled by the possibility that my son could have been saved by potassium replacement therapy. Patients with low potassium and life-threatening heart arrhythmias, which he had, need to have potassium replacement therapy.[5] Parts of his medical records

---

[5] J. N. Cohen, P. R. Kowey, P. K. Whelton, and L. M. Prisant, "New guidelines for potassium replacement in clinical practice," *Arch Intern Med*. 160/16 (2000), 2429–36.

suggested that he had refused a pacemaker, but I knew that his only refusal was for a loop monitor, which was evident in earlier parts of his records. I was further troubled by his medical record missing the results of his cardiac MRI. I became a patient safety advocate.

I often visited the grave of my son. There, I discovered the meaning of the beatitude "Blessed are those who mourn, for they shall be comforted" (Matthew 5:4 NRSV). I learned to mourn at my son's marker with everything I had to pour out of my eyes and heart. I found that about an hour after such deep mourning, I was comforted by a level of peace I had never experienced since his death.

One day in the spring after my son died, I was reading Romans 8 as I sat on a bench in a cypress grove beside a pond from which I could see my son's grave marker. As I read slowly to verse 28, I felt Holy Spirit seize me as certainly as if I had been struck by a large-caliber bullet. I struggle to use words to begin to describe my feeling … It was sudden, certain, and comforting. Holy Spirit led me to know that I must try to stop the harm that happens to those who seek to be healed by medical care, and I was also led to understand that my son was fine but without any deeper insight into what that meant.

In subsequent years, I sustained my faith as a Methodist and participated as an adult in many youth mission trips as well as once going to Haiti during the cholera epidemic that spread after the horrible earthquake in 2011. My eyes were further opened about the inequity of suffering in this world and to the tenacious faith of uneducated, impoverished, and suffering people. I discovered a new kind of love in the Haitian countryside.

My highly educated team worked to move dirt sixty feet from a huge pile and dump it next to the massive concrete foundation of a new church. We used decrepit wheelbarrows to haul the dirt to the foundation. One afternoon, I decided I had had enough of dirt moving, so I offered to give wheelbarrow rides to the children who were steadfastly watching us. I spent most of one hot afternoon loading up to three of them into the wheelbarrow and charging around the complex; I was sustained by their joy, and I gladly neglected the dirt pile.

Near the end of our stay in Haiti, we gathered our stuff together to leave the church area in what turned out to be a decrepit VW bus. As we waited, Melisa, a four-year-old with beautiful, big eyes and a charming, white smile, came up to me. She had been one of my prime wheelbarrow riders. She did not ask; she simply crawled up and sat on my lap until the bus came about forty-five minutes later. At first, I was uncomfortable, but then it dawned on me that she was saying that she would miss me without using words. This was agape love from a child. Perhaps if I had never experienced the loss of a child, I would not have recognized the actions of this small girl as agape.

My journeys through science and religion, mostly Protestantism, have resulted in some reasoned conclusions about what is believable in Christianity and what is unfit to believe. I have been a witness to young people educated in my church who lost all faith when they encountered science in college. Others have fallen into fundamentalism (believing the Bible literally), a form of Christianity that often challenges known, scientific facts and reasoning. My views may outrage some believers, but I ask only that you give time for some of my ideas to sink in. I promise I will not destroy your faith. Indeed, I write this so that your faith may be made stronger by reason, which is one of the four pillars of Methodism (Wesleyan quadrilateral). I ask atheist readers (those who reject a theist god) to give my understanding of God a chance before you continue in disbelief.

I will end each chapter with a prayer for believers and a reflection for nonbelievers. Going into this book, I simply pray that you find something of value.

CHAPTER 1

A GOD WORTHY OF FOLLOWING AS A COMMITTED CHRISTIAN

There are many ideas about the nature of God.[6] Before I begin my challenges to some conventional Christian beliefs, I will try to describe the attributes of a God who embraces our lives as God's children and ambassadors. First, that God must be accessible and welcoming to all persons whether they are children learning right from wrong or old folks hoping for a quick end to this life, whether they are filthy rich or desperately poor, whether they are uneducated or highly educated, whether they are conservative or liberal, whether they are grieving or joyful, or whether they are villains or saints. God must show no favorites and not be arbitrary with gifts.

Given these extremes of life present in the physical world, it should be no surprise that a God who serves this diversity of people will not be tied to worldly happenings or blessings. Indeed, Jesus made it clear that his kingdom, and by extension God's

---

[6] Karen Armstrong, *A History of God* (New York: Ballantine, 1993).

kingdom, is not of this world.[7] Somehow, that God must control a spiritual kingdom that embraces the needs of all people. That God must always be a champion of love, righteousness, empathy, courage, empowerment, justice, truth, forgiveness, and inclusivity. Fear, wrath, anger, vengeance, murder, arrogance, injustice, and worldly favors must play no part in God's actions ever. If your god embraces any of these, please rethink what you believe; you may have been misled.

There is a sweet spot in our spiritual lives where I believe we all can find God as God intended to be discovered. One example of a bridge between science and religion is found in the thinking of Michael Dowd, author of *Thank God for Evolution*. He proposes that evolution is a scared epic that spans 13.8 billion years from creation of the universe to the point now where evolved creatures may contemplate their origins based on scientific evidence. God can be found in the epic of evolution, a story that can be shared by all humankind because it is shared truth at least for scientists. His book was endorsed by five Nobel Prize winners in science and many religious thinkers and leaders.

Scientists know and general observers must recognize that our lives are full of chaos. Indeed, chaos is essential as one of the drivers of biological evolution. In that chaos, genetic mistakes may either favor or disfavor the survival of the next generation. The forces that drive chaos and shape evolutionary success are worldly forces that include man-made disasters such as wars and global warming and natural disasters such as volcano eruptions and earthquakes. It is not in the production of such events that we find

---

[7] "My kingdom is not of this world" (John 18:36).

God; these are not God's specific will. For example, Rev. Franklin Graham's belief that God specifically sent hurricane Katrina in 2005 to punish New Orleans for its many sins is unreasonable.[8] Truthfully, it is in how we respond to such disasters that befall our brothers and sisters that we Christians glorify God as Love. We should not be pointing judgmental fingers.

One troubling mystery of theist Christianity is how there can be so much suffering if God is good and in control. I find an answer to that mystery in understanding that God had to create a world with a general level of suffering for two reasons. First, evolution cannot advance without mistakes that often lead to heartache (genetic diseases) and the demise of entire species that are unable to cope with a changing environment. Second, and perhaps most important, if one accepts that God is Love (1 John 4), then without any suffering, there would be no need for Love and hence no need for God. Imagine if you will a world in which all people are simply delighted each second of their worldly lives (no suffering). Where would God fit into such a world? I posit that it was God's general will that there would be suffering in the chaos of our lives but that God never delivers specific suffering to individuals or selected groups such as the people of New Orleans. Nor does God deliver worldly favors to those who think they are selected for divine favor; the clear message in the New Testament is that God favors no one.

In the days of the COVID-19 pandemic, we observe an

---

evolutionary competition for domination in the world. That competition exists between us presumably intelligent, motivated, and altruistic humans and a tiny virus that seeks to enter our bodies, replicate itself without constraint, and finally kill us. This virus is nothing more than a lifeless, replicating machine that destroys tissue as it seeks domination.

On our side, the question becomes whether we are smart enough to combat this tiny monster with treatments and vaccines. Are we able as the community of humans to sacrifice some of our individual freedoms to ensure that spread of the virus is limited? As I write this, many in the United States are becoming restless about parting with freedoms. Most churches have ceased in-person worship. The counsel of wise and educated medical scientists is being pushed aside for political gain. The virus may yet win because of our selfish, uninformed responses to the pandemic chaos.

True Christians find God in how they respond to chaos and suffering in their and others' lives. We turn our faces and hearts to those who suffer disasters, we seek justice when injustice abounds, and we risk our lives for the well-being of others, but as mere human beings, we are severely limited in our ability to do that. But with Holy Spirit and Christian community as our driving forces, we can do what we would never be able to do alone. The seed of altruism that is naturally in all of us may be only partially expressed until it germinates and grows tall by Holy Spirit. In fact, the apostle John in his first letter concluded that God was Spirit and Love—Agape Love.

Agape love is selfless, sacrificial, and unconditional love. It is the highest of the four types of love in the Bible. It seeks change by demonstrating love through action.[9] The apostle Paul characterized that kind of love in this way.

> Love is patient and kind; love is not jealous or boastful; it is not arrogant or rude. Love does not insist in its own way; it is not irritable or resentful; it does not rejoice at wrong, but rejoices in the right … So, faith, hope and love abide, these three; but the greatest of these is love. (1 Corinthians 13:4–7, 13 RSV)

Please read the whole chapter by the apostle Paul. The God that is Agape Love is worthy of following. I will examine this concept in more depth in chapter 9.

We humans reside in a lonely place in the universe as depicted in Carl Sagan's chracterization of the image of earth seen through the rings of Saturn (fig. 3). We are nothing more than a "pale blue dot." How do we find meaning as one of 7.5 billion humans inhabiting that lonely dot? I think Christianity gives meaning to our lives because it casts us as brothers and sisters working together to preserve our small, vulnerable dot. I will write about this when I consider evolution in more depth.

---

[9] Jack Zavada, March 29, 2018, https://www.thoughtco.com/agape-love-in-the-bible-700675.

Figure 3. The earth photographed by the Cassini spacecraft on July 19, 2013, as seen in the vast distance of our solar system 900 million miles behind the rings of Saturn. The disc of Saturn is obscured in the upper left corner. Carl Sagan dubbed our planet the pale blue dot for obvious reasons. Credit: NASA/JPL-Caltech Space Science Institute.

Prayer: Father God, help us to see the good you placed in all creation through evolution. Make us value all your children living on Carl Sagan's pale blue dot in a solar system in an outer arm of the Milky Way Galaxy. May I know that it is your image that always creates love, goodness, and kindness in us. May I know that our dark side, anger, wrath, injustice, and selfishness are the work of our evil nature, not something we inherited from your image. Empower us through your Holy Spirit to live a life of agape Love. Amen

Reflection: My days are numbered on this earth. I look back and ask, 'when have I failed to live life with love, kindness, and goodness'? When have I caused harm because I was angry, bitter, focused on my prosperity, or on my good times? I must learn from these experiences to change the way I live that I may be part of the wave of humanity that seeks a world of abiding justice with a bright future for all who inhabit Carl Sagan's pale blue dot.

CHAPTER 2

THE BIBLE IS NOT INERRANT

The dogma that the Bible is inerrant or God-breathed simply does not stand up to any reasonable analysis. We find this dogma imbedded in certain Christian traditions. For example, Norman Geisler defines the Bible's inerrancy as "The word inerrancy means not errant, or no error. Biblical inerrancy is the doctrine that says the Bible is without error in all that it affirms."[10] The fact is that the various books of the Bible were written by men with unstable memories and distant in time and place from the events and revelations they sought to describe.

Human memories are notoriously flawed, so the original writing of any book of the Bible is imperfect because those who wrote them depended on memory and oral traditions. Furthermore, all modern Bible editions have been translated by talented people struggling to capture the real meaning of a word when put into another language. Some modern material is highly interpretive rather than faithful to the best-available original texts. One can be sure that the scribes who copied and recopied the texts

---

[10] Bible inerrancy: https://decisionmagazine.com/take-stand-biblical-inerrancy/

in ancient times made mistakes and may have slipped in a few of their own biases. It is a known fact that the original King James Version, despite its elegant language, had "grave defects ... these defects are so many and so serious as to call for a revision of the English translation [of the King James Version]."[11]

▌ In the Beginning

Baptists generally hold that the Bible is uniformly inerrant.[12] A reading of Genesis 1 and Genesis 2–3 and a comparison of the two creation stories there shows that the stories cannot be reconciled with each other. Both cannot be true. In fact, the account in Genesis 1 is remarkably similar in its order to the way scientists understand the creation order of our universe, our planet, and the life that eventually developed here. Is this not a cryptic description of evolution? It also contains the timeless assertion that God created humans in God's image—male and female. To me, this conveys the truth that in all of us is the spiritual ground for righteousness and love.

Obviously, the writer was not present to observe the creation sequence or the first male and female walking around among the plants and animals. Neither of the creation stories in Genesis was meant to be a scientific, factual account. Spiritually, one may deduce from the Genesis 1 account that God is genderless and

---

[11] Preface to the Holy Bible, Revised Standard Version (New York: Thomas Nelson, 1953), iii.

[12] Bible Baptist Church, https://www.bbcv.org/beliefs.

that men and women are spiritually equal, both sharing God's spiritual image.

Some might argue that while there is nothing factual in the Genesis 2–3 creation story, there is truth in it. By truth, it is meant that the reader discovers insights that are not subject to factual analysis but are a biblical affirmation (per Geisler). This is the Adam and Eve story in which God warns Adam to not try to capture knowledge of good and evil by eating from a certain tree. But alas, Adam needed a helper, so God created a woman from Adam's body to become that helper. Now in Genesis 3, the woman was warned in Adam's presence not to seek knowledge of good and evil by eating from this tree. But she wanted to become wise like God, so she ate of the fruit and gave some to clueless Adam. Both became aware of their nakedness and donned appropriate covering. What truth may be made of this story?

We can query the New Testament to see the supposed truth the apostle Paul made of it in one of his letters. In 1 Timothy 2:11–14 (NRSV), he wrote,

> Let a woman learn in silence with full submission. I permit no woman to teach or have authority over a man; she is to keep silent. For Adam was formed first, then Eve; and Adam was not deceived, but the woman was deceived and became a transgressor.

So the truth Paul found in his biased interpretation of the Genesis 2–3 story was that women are to be subordinated to men. This may have been a truth at the time Genesis 2–3 or 1 Timothy was written, but these days, it is certainly not a truth to anyone but Christian misogynists. It is a time-dated truth that has no lasting value as the truth from Genesis 1 does: men and women were created in the spiritual image of God. That is timeless and factual because we know that human beings are capable of sacrificial love just as God demonstrated when God became incarnate as Jesus.

The above passage was followed by these words attributed to Paul (1 Timothy 11:15, NRSV): "Yet she will be saved through childbearing provided they continue in faith and love and holiness, with modesty." This is a truly awful assertion at first impressions. I recall with a taste of outrage the evening when we in a Disciple I Bible study class came across this passage. A young woman in the class burst into tears because she knew she was unlikely to marry and unlikely to bear a child. Did this exclude her from salvation? We in the class assured her that childbearing was not a prerequisite to salvation, that Paul was just kidding.

So why are the Genesis 1 and Genesis 2–3 accounts of human creation so different? The first comes from the priestly or P tradition in which God is called Elohim in ancient Hebrew whereas the second comes from the Yahwist tradition. Our Old Testament is thought to be a weaving together of these traditional understandings of God and two others, but of course, the theologians continue to argue about this. Yahweh became the warrior god of the ancient Hebrews purportedly leading them to many victories over their enemies. It is not reasonable to assert that such an understanding of God is compatible with the understanding Jesus gave us of his Father. In fact, many of the Jews of Jesus's time were expecting a warrior Messiah, but instead, they were given a peace-loving, radically kind, humble man from Nazareth, a country village far from Jerusalem.

▌ Marcion's Canon

Most Christians are never told that the first Christian canon appeared about 150 CE and was based on the gospel of Luke (minus Jesus's birth story) and most of Paul's letters.[13] It specifically did not include the Hebrew scriptures that we now label the Old Testament. In fact, Marcion's canon specifically rejected the Old Testament as the story of an evil god. The canon was attributed to Marcion, who felt that Christianity was pure love.

Marcionites thrived well into the third century, but when Constantine forced Christians to come up with a list of canonical books of the Bible, the Hebrew scriptures were included as the Old Testament, and the God of the Old Testament (primarily Yahweh) was deemed to be the same as the God of the Greek scriptures (Jesus's Father). I struggled with this for many years because the behavior attributed to God in the Old Testament is often incompatible with the behavior of Jesus in the New Testament. Initially when I learned all this, I tended to lean toward Marcion's belief that the Hebrew scriptures were the tale of an evil god, yet in the Old Testament, I saw spiritual passion and prophesy (teaching) pointing to the New Testament understanding of God. For example,

> I will pour out my spirit on all flesh; your sons and your daughters shall prophesy, your old men shall dream dreams, your young men shall see visions. Even

---

[13] Lee M. McDonald, *The Formation of the Christian Biblical Canon*, Peabody, MA: Hendrickson, 2005), 154–61.

on the male and female slaves, in those days, I will
pour out my spirit. (Joel 2:28–29 NRSV)

There had to be a middle ground between Marcion's view and
orthodoxy that currently insists on biblical inerrancy.

After much reasoning and frustration, I concluded that the
Old Testament God and New Testament God are the same;
however, the *understanding* of God matured from the days of
the Old Testament until Jesus came to give direct personal
witness to God's true nature. In fact, it is reasonable to think
that Jesus was sent to correct the gross misunderstandings of God
portrayed in the Old Testament. Let me put this bluntly: If you
believe that the Bible is the inerrant Word of God, you believe
in a God who drowned everyone in the world in anger (Genesis
6:2–8:22), repeatedly hardened Pharaoh's heart (Exodus 4:21,
7:3, 9:12), committed genocide against the ancient Egyptians
(Exodus 12:29), sent a great plague on people who ate quail
(Numbers 31–33), established rules of war that demanded total
annihilation of villages (Deuteronomy 20:16), repeatedly sent
evil spirits on Saul (1 Samuel 16:14, 18:10, 19:9), colluded with
Satan to kill Job's children (Job 1:12, 18–19), forced David's wives
to commit adultery as penance for his adultery with Bathsheba
(2 Samuel 12:11–12), prescribed stoning to death for rebellious
boys (Deuteronomy 21:18–21), sent plagues that killed tens of
thousands of innocent people (2 Samuel 24:1–17), and sent Jacob
to annihilate all that breathed in villages in the land the Jews
claimed as promised to them (Joshua 10:40). By any reasonable
standard, these are evil deeds believed by the writers of the Old
Testament to have been perpetrated by God. The ancient Jews

wanted a powerful and worldly God who would deliver victories in battle, so they tended to understand God in those terms.

One notes a growing awareness as one reads the Old Testament prophets that this idea of a worldly war god is going to change dramatically to one of heart and Spirit (Ezekiel 36:26–27; Joel 2:28–29) as it indeed does when Jesus became God incarnate (or the Son of God) bearing the true wisdom and reason (*logos* in Greek, John 1) of God to humans.

Yahweh's Curse on Women

Now using a scientific perspective, let us consider one of Yahweh's earliest punishments, this one given to women after the episode in the garden. The forbidden fruit was eaten by Adam and Eve. The writer must have been aware that women of his day experienced severe pain while giving birth compared to other creatures in the ancient Hebrew environment. He must have deduced that women had done something to stir the wrath of Yahweh to experience such pain with each birth. So he concocted a story to explain why women had to endure extreme pain during delivery of a baby. The scientific truth is that women ambulate on two legs, and to do that efficiently, they must have relatively narrow hips compared to four-legged animals. In addition, the heads of human babies are large compared to the heads of other mammals at birth. According to the modern obstetrical understanding, it is the combination of a moderately narrow birth canal and large head that elicits pain as the mother's muscles must repeatedly contract with great strength to push the baby through a narrow opening.[14] I cannot reasonably accept that a loving God would curse all women with extreme pain during childbirth (Genesis 3:16). The same declaration of pain during birth also included the edict that the man shall rule over the woman, an unfortunate theme that is never fully reversed in the Bible.

▌ Many Gods of the Bible

Monotheism, or lack thereof, is also an issue in the beliefs expressed in the Christian Old Testament. I would never have gleaned this by reading the Hebrew scriptures, but scholars who spend time on this sort of thing have noticed that the idea of a single, universal God is not apparent until well into the book of Isaiah.[15] The ancient Hebrews were surrounded by tribes that believed in different gods, and to some extent, those beliefs periodically affected the beliefs of the Hebrews. For example, if one reads the declaration of the commandments given by Moses upon his descent from the mountain, one notes that the first commandment declared that there would be multigenerational punishment for anyone who had another god before Yahweh (Exodus 20:3–6), whereas well into Isaiah, one reads, "Thus says Yahweh, Israel's king, Yahweh Sabaoth, his redeemer; I am the first and I am the last; there is no God except me" (Isaiah 44:6 NJB). So the scientist in me asks, if the writers of the oldest parts of the Old Testament

---

[14] https://www.americanscientist.org/article/why-is-human-childbirth-so-painful.
[15] https://claudemariottini.com/2013/09/23/monotheism-and-the-faith-of-israel/.

15

did not clearly understand that there was one and only one God, how could they have accurately characterized the true nature of that God? This might be likened to ancient astronomers trying to understand our solar system with the naked eye before Galileo's discoveries with a telescope in the early 1600s. For example, Johannes Kepler, despite his substantial astronomical discoveries, was still trying to find music in the motions of heavenly bodies as late as 1619.[16] There is no music. It was his imagination. There is only one God. The others are imaginations.

I discovered that I was not alone in my struggles with the incompatibilities of the Old and New Testaments. After my son died, a cousin of my mother's sent me a Cokesbury Bible that had three ways to view the authority of the Bible.[17] The first is that it is a story of salvation history in which God is involved. As I described above, the horrible acts attributed to God in the Old Testament are nothing short of raw fearmongering, not an acceptable characteristic of a righteous God. That is not a reasonable way to see God unless one wishes to reject Jesus's Father, in which case one cannot call oneself a Christian.

The second way to understand the Bible is called the Christocentric view, first attributed to Martin Luther. Anything in the Old Testament or other sources that disagreed with the words of Jesus did not have equal authority with Jesus's teachings. I would go further and claim that if something disagreed with Jesus's teachings, it had no authority.

The third means of understanding biblical authority is the effect

---

[16] http://adsabs.harvard.edu/full/2003JRASC..97..228G.
[17] Cokesbury Bible, NRSV (Nashville: Thomas Nelson, 1990), 4–5.

Bible reading has on the reader. This is a form of existentialism, the philosophical idea emphasizing individual existence as one grows responsibly and exercises free will accordingly. This is an important basis of authority. As I explained in the prologue, it was as I was reading Romans 8 that I was first and most certainly indwelled by Holy Spirit. And that has freed me from the shackles of unreasoned belief.

I was delighted to discover that the Rev. Adam Hamilton, a remarkably successful United Methodist preacher leading the Church of the Resurrection near Kansas City, Kansas, also encourages his many followers to take the Christocentric view of the Bible. In one of his videos, he uses a colander to sift for truth.[18] The colander represents New Testament truth. If one places the Old Testament understandings of God in the colander, only those teachings that were consistent with Jesus's teaching would be held in the colander of truth about God. Mischaracterizations fall through and are left as chaff, meaning they were not true, timeless revelations from or about God.

Allow me to add one additional biblical story concerning God's Spirit to compare the understandings in each testament. In Judges 11:29–39, the Spirit of Yahweh came to Jephthah, and he vowed that if he won the battle with the Ammonites, when he returned in triumph to his house, he would sacrifice the first thing that came out of his door. Yahweh was apparently faithful to the vow because the Ammonites were defeated. When Jephthah returned home, his daughter, his only child, was the first to come out of the house.

---

[18] A. Hamilton, "Wrestling with the Bible," sermon series August 19, 2012 to September 16, 2012, United Methodist Church of the Resurrection, Leawood, KS.

Jephthah confessed that that made him miserable, but he would not break his vow to Yahweh. His daughter asked only that she be allowed two months to be free with her friends and mourn that she would never be married. Her wish was granted, and upon her return, Jephthah killed her in accord with his vow to give Yahweh a burnt offering. Curiously, Hebrews 11:32 seems to honor Jephthah's faith in this story. Jesus made it clear that vows were not to be taken (Matthew 5:33–37). Jephthah's daughter was the victim of a horrible misunderstanding of God as Yahweh, the giver of victories in battle.

If your stomach can stand it, you can learn more about burnt offerings from the story of Abraham and Isaac as Abraham was asked by Yahweh to sacrifice his son as a burnt offering (Genesis 22:1–12). Father and son trudged up the mountain where a pyre was built, and Isaac was placed on it. Abraham was about to slit the boy's throat with a knife when his hand was stilled by an angel of Yahweh. A ram appeared and was substituted for Isaac. According to the story of the daughter of Jephthah, her father's hand was not stilled. Some years ago, I attended a bar mitzvah. The rabbi delivered an interesting sermon referring to the Abraham and Isaac story in which he made it clear that no righteous God would ever ask a man to murder his son.

The Synoptic Problem

The New Testament is not free of conflicting accounts of the events of Jesus's ministry. Years ago, when I was passing time in a consignment shop, I found a collection of books that must have belonged to a deceased minister. Among them was a colorful book called *A History of the Synoptic Problem* by David Laird Dungan, a distinguished professor of humanities at the University of Tennessee.[19] I parted with $6 and read most of Dungan's book.

Origen in the early 200s was perhaps the first to deal with the problem of inconsistencies in the accounts of Jesus in Matthew, Mark, and Luke. Which were true records of the ministry of Jesus? Which versions of the four trusted gospels should be used? How did the gospels depend on each other? And why do stories common to each differ so much? Finally, Origen asks, "How does one distil truth, literal or spiritual, from the stories?" Dungan traced a variety of issues associated with the interpretation of the Gospels and how to deal with their original sources, their differences, and their interdependence, and which was composed first. One important issue is the dating of the gospel of John (not a synoptic gospel). The prevailing opinion is that it was written last, perhaps as late as 90 CE. I have a book by Paul Barnett, a former Anglican bishop of North Sydney, Australia,[20] in which he makes what seems to me to be a reasonable case that the gospel of John was the first to be written and independently of the synoptic gospels perhaps as early as 30–60 CE. The assertions made in the gospel of John are much different from those of the synoptics. For example, it is only in John's gospel that Jesus is called God incarnate. Moreover, John offered a fresh creation story to start his understanding of Jesus and God. Light has come into darkness!

---

[19] David Laird Dungan, *A History of the Synoptic Problem* (New York: Doubleday, 1999) 65-88

[20] Paul Barnett, *The Birth of Christianity—The First Twenty Years* (Grand Rapids, MI: Eerdmans, 2005), 163–79.

▓ Biblical Interpretation

Given all this, how does a mere layperson reasonably interpret the Bible? Start by knowing what it is. It is a collection of writings often by unknown authors who sought to understand the nature of God in the context of the times in which they lived. The books were typically written centuries after the events described (Old Testament) or decades after the events described (New Testament).

As times changed, the biblical understanding of God changed culminating in the teachings of Jesus and his apostles. Jesus came to fulfill the law (Matthew 5:17), which in fact means that he came to "bring it forth in truth." Although Jesus was an observant Jew, he was not shy about blasting the beliefs of his time and clarifying that salvation was by faith, not by following some set of rules. As Christians, our purpose is to love others and especially those who are suffering and those with whom we share animosity. Rather than drill into a multitude of passages from the Bible, we should look for fundamental, timeless understandings of God. We must trust that all we need to know about God to live our lives is revealed in the New Testament. Yet even in the New Testament, we must be wary of time-trapped beliefs such as the behavior toward slaves and women.

The scientist in me wants to make an analogy between our historical understanding of God's nature and the historical understanding of our earth. That understanding has evolved from flat earth to round earth (ancient Greeks), to earth revolving around the sun (Galileo), to the sun being part of the Milky Way Galaxy (Hubble), and finally to a realization that the universe, full of a great many galaxies, can be measured only in light-years of distance. We are indeed living on Carl Sagan's miniscule pale blue dot. Somehow for me, this lonely perspective is mitigated by the ultimate spiritual understanding that God is Love (1 John 4). It took humankind millennia to discover our true place in the universe, and it has taken millennia for us to understand the true nature of God to the extent we need to understand it. Flat-earth Christianity has no place in the mind of a reasoning Christian.

As I was wrapping up this chapter, a friend loaned me a book called *The Historical Jesus for Beginners* by William M. Linden, who is not a formally trained theologian.[21] The historical Jesus's workshop attempted to use scholarly methods to discern which of the sayings attributed to Jesus in the gospels were authentic. The analysis assumed that the noncanonical book of Thomas was part of the legitimate collections of Jesus's sayings, and it acknowledged that Matthew and Luke depended on lost, early writings such as M or Q. The key criterion for acceptance of authenticity is that a saying must appear in more than one independent source. The so-called independent sources have layers (written material added over time). This approach dramatically distilled the sayings of Jesus, and it left out sayings and stories in the gospel of John because it was assumed to have been written much later than the other gospels. The writer of John was too theologically sophisticated to contain original, authentic sayings of Jesus it was claimed.

As a scientist, I think that the attempt to uncover Jesus's authentic sayings has one serious weakness. It is likely that many

---

[21] William M. Linden, *The Historical Jesus for Beginners* (Eugene, OR: Wipf & Stock, 2008).

primary sources for his sayings were created but that most of these were lost over time. What we have today is a small sample of what must have been a sizeable number of primary sayings, some oral and others written down and later lost.

The one understanding I like in Linden's book is in his last chapter, "The Spirit of the Historical Jesus." Here, Linden declares that the historical sayings must be combined with the Spirit of Jesus, which is captured in the gospel of John and associated letters. Therein lies the Spirit of the historical Jesus, and this is where we must focus. Is there a way to simplify our understanding of the Bible by placing our focus on the gospel of John and associated letters? I think there is. Is there a Christian theological equivalent to Newton's law of motion, $F = ma$, or Einstein's theory of relativity expressed as $E = mc^2$?[22]

For those of you who have been taught to believe that the Bible is the uniformly inerrant Word of God, I ask only that you apply unbiased reasoning to the biblical stories. I do not mean to destroy your trust in the Bible but to offer a more reasonable way to understand it. Everyone and every Christian picks and chooses what he or she wishes to believe. I have chosen to believe that the Bible builds truth stories until it reaches the mountaintop of truth, where God is understood by the apostle John as Love and (Holy) Spirit (1 John 4). It is important to understand that this is agape love: selfless, sacrificial, unconditional, and impelled to action. agape love is the first gift of Holy Spirit (Galatians 5). It is that simple. To put this in quasi-scientific terms, remember that

---

[22] Force equals mass times acceleration, and energy equals mass times the speed of light squared.

Jesus has gone from our pale blue dot: God = Agape Love + Holy Spirit. More on these subjects will come in subsequent chapters.

▌ Agape

For those of you who see yourselves as atheists or agnostics, I ask only that you examine your lives to discern if you have received or inadvertently given agape love. Perhaps you have experienced God without being aware of God's presence. Agape love might be characterized as altruism on steroids. This is generally not the view of God that most atheists have rejected. For me, all the religious creeds, sacraments, dogma, doctrine, rules, and prohibitions are secondary to the understanding that God is Agape.

A few years ago, I heard a minister state in his sermon, "What we do in church is like the huddle in football—it prepares us for the real action on the field outside church walls where it counts." As a Christian mystic, I do not need church, but I realize that I do value the huddles with my brothers and sisters that make me better able to project agape outside the brick walls. Christianity without placing agape foremost is counterfeit. Secular life lived without agape is life not fully lived.

Prayer: Father God, help me to use the reasoning ability I have developed over my lifetime to intelligently examine the ancient words of the Bible, understanding that it reflects the times in which it was written. Help me identify those passages that are timeless and fully consistent with New Testament truths. Enable me to discern through Holy Spirit where the nature of God was misunderstood by the writer, that I may not be misled into hopeless confusion about your nature. Help me find fundamental biblical truths that will guide my biblical understanding. Amen

Reflection: Perhaps I should be curious about this collection of books called "Holy Bible." In the past when I examined it, I found stories that appalled me. Maybe I have relied too much on the interpretation of others than on my own reasoning ability. Should I take another look, this time finding the *relevant* stories that inspire me to live a better life? Even if I do not believe in Yahweh, I would like to be more like the Good Samaritan and less like the Priest and Levite who did (Luke 10:25-37).

CHAPTER 3

WOMEN IN CHURCH LEADERSHIP

The bias against women in church leadership is a long-standing practice in many Christian traditions. Two that come to mind are the Roman Catholic and Southern Baptist. Is this a reasonable practice, or has it come from the historical dominance of men in various cultures and in religious sects? Cultural dominance has included physical and scholarly dominance as men had control of what was recorded in the Bible and other religious documents. One is not much challenged to find instances in the Old Testament in which women were regarded as grossly inferior to men.[23]

In the New Testament, we observe clear indications from Paul that women were to be subordinated to men in church affairs.[24] To me, this and other scriptures like it are time-bound declarations, which means they do not apply to our times. I suspect Paul wanted as much stability in his church plants as

---

[23] J. Walker, *The Dark Bible. Women's Inferior Status* (2006), https://spiritual-minds.com/religion/christianity/darkbible/TheDarkBibl.pdf
[24] Tom McAnally, http://ee.umc.org/what-we-believe/commentary-why-do-united-methodists-ordain-women.

possible, so going along with the common Jewish traditions of subordinating women was convenient and avoided another break with tradition that was unnecessary for those times.

Few Jewish religious texts have provoked as much indignation and discomfort as the brief passage that is recited by traditional Jewish men at the beginning of their daily morning prayers: "Blessed are you, Lord, our God, ruler of the universe who has not created me a woman."[25] In addition, women were emphatically excluded from the inner court, where Israelite men gathered for religious activities (sacrifices) in the Jerusalem temple of Jesus's time.[26] Those times are long past, and apologists of today offer various ways to deny that this prayer and exclusivity by men reflected the attitude of Jewish males in Jesus's time.

▓ Women Leaders in the New Testament

Despite Paul's admonition against women in church leadership, there is reasonable evidence that they were in fact involved in church leadership. Bart Ehrman, chair of the Department of Religion at the University of North Carolina at Chapel Hill, whose ideas often challenge orthodox doctrine, provides a compelling case for at least a few women leaders in the early church.[27] Here, I will describe some of his more convincing examples and add one

---

[25] This prayer comes from the Talmud, which was in an oral form in Paul's times before 70 CE, https://www.myjewishlearning.com/article/who-has-not-made-me-a-woman/, https://en.wikipedia.org/wiki/Talmud.

[26] https://www.bible-history.com/court-of-women/.

[27] Bart D. Ehrman, *Misquoting Jesus* (San Francisco: Harper, 2005), 178–86.

I think is more important than anything we find in Paul's letters. In Romans 16:7 (NRSV), Paul declared, "Greet Andronicus and Junia [a woman], my relatives who were in prison with me; they are prominent among the apostles, and they were in Christ before I was." Similarly, from Romans 16:1 (NRSV), "I commend to you our sister Phoebe, a deacon of the church at Cenchreae." Clearly, in Galatians 3:25–28 (NRSV), there is a new and timeless standard for the relationships between believers.

> But now that faith has come, we are no longer subject to a disciplinarian [the Law], for in Christ Jesus you are all children of God through faith. As many of you as were baptized into Christ have clothed yourselves with Christ. There is no longer Jew or Greek, there is no longer slave or free, there is no longer male or female; for all are one in Christ Jesus.

Note (Ephesians 6:5; Colossians 3:22) that Paul admonished slaves to "obey your earthly masters." Like the subordination of women, this decree on slavery is of the time it was written and should have no standing in modern Christian doctrine.

Herein I will add one further biblical example in which a woman was a leader. Evangelical Christians that insist on keeping women out of leadership would do well to review the story of the Samaritan woman Jesus met at the well as described in John 4:1–42. This is by far the longest story in the gospel of John. It tells of the encounter between a scorned woman living in Sychar, Samaria, and Jesus. This woman had had five husbands and was living with a man. Jesus told her that worshippers would worship the Father in Spirit and truth. Because of Jesus's insights into her past, she believed that Jesus was the anticipated Messiah. Just then, his disciples returned wondering why he was talking with a woman. Proper Jewish males did not do that, nor did they speak with Samaritans. With her exciting news, the woman rushed back to her village and recruited many to come see Jesus, the Messiah.

The story continues (John 4:39–42 RSV).

> Many Samaritans from that city believed in him [Jesus] because of the woman's testimony. "He told me all that I ever did." So, when the Samaritans came to him, they asked him to stay with them; and he stayed there 2 days. And many more believed because of his word. They said to the woman, "It is no longer because of your words that we believe, for we have heard for ourselves, and we know that this is indeed the Savior of the World."

The first Christian evangelist was a woman, and a scorned Samaritan at that.

This story follows on the heels of the story of Jesus's encounter with Nicodemus in Jerusalem (John 3:1–21). Nicodemus was a leader of the Jews, a Pharisee. Jesus rather bluntly questioned why he did not understand the need to be born again not in the physical sense from a woman but born from above by Holy Spirit. Here, Jesus likened Holy Spirit to the wind. One senses its presence, but where it is coming from and where it is going are a mystery. The stark contrast in John's gospel between the Samaritan woman's simple and sudden belief in Jesus as Messiah and the Pharisee's lack of insight seems intentional and obvious to me.

One other story from the Gospels suggests an important influence a woman may have had on Jesus's ministry. As the story goes in Matthew 15:21–28, Jesus had withdrawn to the area of Tyre and Sidon, villages north of Samaria along the Mediterranean coast. A Canaanite woman was begging for mercy from Jesus. Canaan designates a land conquered or destroyed by Joshua's Yahweh-directed invasion of the area of Palestine. The woman's daughter was suffering from demon possession. Jesus ignored her noting that he was sent only to the lost sheep of Israel. Kneeling, she pleaded for Jesus's help. He said he would not toss the children's bread to their dogs. But, she pleaded, the dogs can eat the crumbs that fall beneath the table. Jesus, noting her great faith, granted that her daughter be healed. The same story is told in similar form in Mark 7:24–30. It is reasonable to me to suppose that these stories were an affirmation of Paul's ministry to the Gentiles after Jesus was crucified. They got the crumbs, but oh what crumbs they were!

▌ Women Gain Leadership

Although United Methodists formally disallowed women in ministry until 1956, apparently, John Wesley, the founder of Methodism, allowed at least one woman, Sarah Crosby, to be ordained to preach in 1761.[28]

One of the best sermons I ever heard was delivered by Rev. Sandra Stephens in the Father Dyer United Methodist Church in Breckenridge, Colorado, in August 1993. Her sermon included thoughtful insights into how Methodists should feel about the

---

[28] Why does the United Methodist church ordain women? https://www.umc.org/en/content/ask-the-umc-why-does-the-united-methodist-church-ordain-women

visit of Pope John Paul II to Denver.[29] She was respectful of our Roman Catholic brothers and sisters but embraced the different doctrines that Methodists had adopted, obviously one of which was to allow women in church leadership.

It seems that ordination of women as deacons in the Roman Catholic church may have a small chance under Pope Francis.[30] As I write this, the Roman Catholic Church is being consumed by new waves of sordid revelations. Pedophile priests have been protected by the church for many years, and some in high leadership are involved. There are calls to allow male priests to marry and for women to be allowed to become priests. In fact, a movement to ordain women priests began in Germany in 2002 and appears to be spreading despite high-level resistance and low-level scorn.[31] Roman Catholics insist on not ordaining women because it was a "deposit of faith." A dictionary defined "deposit of faith" as the body of revealed truth in the scriptures and tradition proposed by the Roman Catholic Church for the belief of the faithful.[32] This was most emphatically declared by Pope John Paul II in 1994.[33]

---

[29] *LA Times*, August 4, 1993: http://articles.latimes.com/1993-08-04/news/mn-20349_1_security-fund.

[30] J. Manson, "It's time to be honest about Pope Francis and Women," National Catholic Reporter Blog, May 19, 2016, https://www.ncronline.org/blogs/grace-margins/its-time-be-honest-about-pope-francis-and-women.

[31] https://www.irishcentral.com/news/women-priests-catholic. The story of the beginning of the ordination of women as priests is told in *Vogue* magazine of all places: https://www.vogue.com/projects/13543313/roman-catholic-women-priest-movement-giulia-bianchi/.

[32] https://www.merriam-webster.com/dictionary/deposit%20of%20faith.

[33] Deposit of faith Pope John Paul II 1994. 2019: https://www.ncregister.com/blog/john-paul-ii-definitively-said-no-to-women-priests

Please ask yourself if subordination of women by church doctrine is reasonable.

One interesting personal insight comes from the only president I ever met. It was on a commercial flight. He and his Secret Service detail were headed to the back of the coach section. He walked past me, and through my shock, I recognized him. I finally uttered, "President Carter." He turned back up the aisle to shake my hand and say hello. This humble former president was flying coach! President Carter broke with the Southern Baptist Church over the issue of equality of women.[34] He understood that the basis of bias against women being lead pastors in churches came from Paul's time-bound opinions in forming and stabilizing the early church plants. It is time bound and inappropriate to apply misogyny to church leadership today.

▌ Unique Gifts of Women

We males would do well to ask what women might bring to the pulpit that we could never bring. As a man, have you ever felt new life move inside your body? Have you ever wept as the new life that just emerged from your body lost all signs of life? Have you ever held a baby as she eagerly nursed and felt the love that unites a mother and baby? Have you ever been sexually abused or horribly beaten by a powerful man who cannot control his sexual urges or anger? Are you a woman sick of the mass killings by men? Since 1982 through July 2022, of the one-hundred-and-thirty mass

---

[34] ABC News, "Jimmy Carter leaves Southern Baptists," https://abcnews. go.com/US/story?id=95311&page=1.

killings in the US by individuals, all but three were committed by men.[35] Are we males so arrogant that we refuse to listen to women speak to us from a position of church leadership?

One attribute that must be brought to church leadership is compassion. Based on a poll by Pew Research Center, Americans clearly see women as far more compassionate than men (fig. 4). In addition, they are perceived as more organized and honest than men. We males score high on ambition and deciseveness. I view Jesus's ministry as one of exceptional compassion for the marginalized and suffering. He was decisively opposed to the religious hierarchy of his time.

One can trace the nature of the people Jesus healed in Matthew 8–9. There, we read reports of the healing of a leper, a centurian's servant, Peter's mother-in-law, a paralytic, two blind men, and a mute person. In Matthew 9:36–7 (RSV), we read, "When he [Jesus] saw the crowds, he had compassion for them, because they were harrassed and helpless, like sheep without a shepherd." Perhaps if we were to welcome more women into church leadership, the church would change to become more compassionate; in fact, this might lead more men to become compassionate, which some may see as going against natural tendencies of most males.

---

[35] https://www.statista.com/statistics/476445/mass-shootings-in-the-us-by-shooter-s-gender/

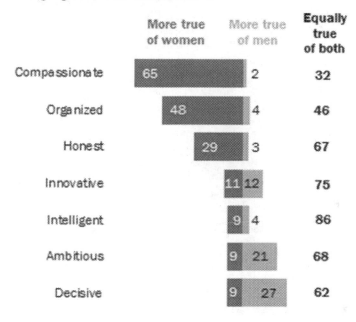

Women Seen as More Compassionate, Men More Decisive

% saying each characteristic is ...

	More true of women	More true of men	Equally true of both
Compassionate	65	2	32
Organized	48	4	46
Honest	29	3	67
Innovative	11	12	75
Intelligent	9	4	86
Ambitious	9	21	68
Decisive	9	27	62

Note: "No answer" not shown.

Source: Pew Research Center survey, Nov. 12-21, 2014 (N=1,835)

PEW RESEARCH CENTER   Q7a-g

Figure 4: Survey by the Pew Research Center comparing the characteristics of men and women.[36]

In these times, women are capturing enough power to become presidents, heads of state, and prime ministers of major countries.

[36] https://www.pewresearch.org/wp-content/uploads/sites/3/2015/01/2015-01-14_women-and-leadership_main-topline.pdf.

JOHN T. JAMES, PhD

Since World War II, scores of women have led major countries around the world for more than one year. A partial list includes the following.[37]

Indira Gandhi (India, 1966–77, 1980–84)

Soong Ching-ling (China, 1968–72)

Golda Meir (Israel, 1969–74)

Isabel Martínez de Perón (Argentina, 1974–76)

Margaret Thatcher (United Kingdom, 1979–90)

Milka Planinc (Yugoslavia, 1982–86)

Jeanne Sauvé (Canada, 1984–90)

Benazir Bhutto (Pakistan, 1988–90, 1993–96)

Violeta Chamorro (Nicaragua, 1990–97)

Gro Harlem Brundtland (Norway, 1990–96)

Mary Robinson (Ireland, 1990–97)

Khaleda Zia (Bangladesh, 1991–96, 2001–06)

Hanna Suchocka (Poland, 1992–93)

Tansu Çiller (Turkey, 1993–96)

Sheikh Hasina (Bangladesh, 1996–2001)

Mary McAleese (Ireland (1997–2011)

Mireya Moscoso (Panama, 1999–2004)

Adrienne Clarkson (Canada, 1999–2005)

Tarja Halonen (Finland, 2000–12)

Megawati Sukarnoputri (Indonesia, 2001–04)

Luísa Diogo (Mozambique, 2004–10)

Michaëlle Jean (Canada, 2005–10)

[37] https://en.wikipedia.org/wiki/List_of_elected_and_appointed_female_heads_of_state_and_government.

Angela Merkel (Germany, 2005–18)
Michelle Bachelet (Chile, 2006–10)
Pratibha Patil (India, 2007–12)
Cristina Fernández de Kirchner (Argentina, 2007–15)
Yulia Tymoshenko (Ukraine, 2007–10)
Dame Quentin Bryce (Australia, 2008–14)
Sheikh Hasina (Bangladesh, 2009–18)

The list goes on, but this is more than sufficient. The reason I gave this long list is to emphasize the geographical diversity of countries headed by women. I have excluded some small countries such as Switzerland, New Zealand, Philippines, and South Korea. The United States has never been headed by a woman. It is reasonable to observe that if a woman can lead a major country, a woman can certainly lead a church. They were created in the image of God.

Although I remain critical of the bias against women in the leadership of some Christian traditions, I recognize that most men in these traditions do not consider women to be inferior as suggested by some biblical ideas. These men fully respect women but rightly view them as different on average. However, if one were to objectively measure the ability of the two sexes to be organized, there would be a mean level of organization and a distribution for each of the sexes. There would be overlap in the distributions such that many well-organized men would in fact be more organized than some poorly organized women. Given such overlaps in social attributes, it makes no sense to me to claim that women could never make excellent pastors, bishops, cardinals, and popes.

▌ Darkness

In my white, middle-class, business-oriented culture, I observe that men are becoming more compassionate and women in leadership positions more decisive. In my opinion, if all church traditions embraced women in top leadership, there would be fewer destructive, darkness-shrouded revelations. As I write this, these revelations now include a scandal in the Southern Baptist Church over failure to discipline men in leadership who were documented sexual predators,[38] and in the Roman Catholic Church, it is coming to light that priests may have been disregarding their chastity vows with nuns who subsequently became pregnant.[39] One may posit that if these church traditions had embraced women participating at the highest levels of leadership, there would at least have been less of this predatory behavior. It is obvious from the #Me Too movement that mixing men and women in an environment where men have the power over women is a recipe for misbehavior, whereas the reverse is rarely the case. I cannot think of one case where a powerful woman has been accused of demanding sexual favors from subordinate men excepting possibly Catherine the Great.[40]

As I was wrapping up the first draft of this book, I was shocked to discover darkness reflected in an article in *JAMA Internal Medicine.* It assessed the adverse health effects on young American women who had been forced by men to engage in sex as their

---

[38] https://www.houstonchronicle.com/news/investigations/article/Southern-Baptist-sexual-abuse-spreads-as-leaders-13588038.php.

[39] https://apnews.com/f7ec3cec9a4b46868aa584fe1c94fb28.

[40] https://www.biography.com/news/catherine-the-great-lovers.

initiation into that activity.[41] My shock was not so much about the adverse health effects on women, which included unwanted pregnancy, endometriosis, and inflammatory pelvic disease. What shocked me most was the prevalence of forced sexual initiation and the early age at which this occurs. The authors estimated that more than 3 million American women between the ages of 18 and 44 have experienced forced sexual initiation and that the average age at initiation was 15½ years. For women not forced into initiation of sex, the average age at first sexual experience was 17½ years. The message to me is that our culture still has a long way to go before men fully respect women.

Our churches should lead in this effort by giving women more power to exert their free wills to be leaders in the churches and to bring up girls to know that they can say no to men who are trying to force their will on them. Unwelcome sexual initiation on young women in America is one of the great injustices that needs correction by churches. This will be difficult to accomplish while church leaders turn a blind eye to sexual predators and keep women from leadership roles.

Pioneering Women

A suitable conclusion to this chapter is to share stories of women breaking down barriers. The history of female leadership in Protestant churches is interesting. Ruth Perry compiled a list of

---

[41] L. Hawks et al., "Association between forced sexual initiation and health outcomes among American women," https://jamanetwork.com/journals/jamainternalmedicine/article-abstract/2751247.

ten awesome women preachers. The stories of these women show remarkable courage, unbridled compassion, long ministries, and pioneering spirits.[42] United Methodist women are remarkably active in my denomination now constituting about a fourth of ordained pastors.[43]

I found an interesting quote from a site featuring black women preachers. Sojourner Truth, who escaped from plantation slavery in 1828 and became an itinerant preacher in New York City, was quoted as reinterpreting the Bible as follows.

> Then that little man [preacher] in black there, he says women can't have as much rights as men, because Christ wasn't a woman! Where did your Christ come from? From God and a woman! Man had nothing to do with Him.[44]

With her words, I rest my case for women in church leadership.

---

[42] https://www.cbeinternational.org/blogs/10-awesome-women-pastors-history.

[43] http://www.umc.org/topics/topic-women-in-leadership.

[44] http://theconversation.com/hidden-figures-how-black-women-preachers-spoke-truth-to-power-73185.

Prayer. Holy Spirit of the living God remind me always that those of the opposite sex are, like me, made in your Spiritual image. Though we may be different in our outward properties, we are equally children of God. May we always be the hand of God to each other, always treating each other with agape love. May we seek always to eliminate the injustices that subordinate women in the church and in our society. Amen

Reflection. Sometimes the opposite sex confounds me with its perplexing behavior and needs. I want to understand those attributes better, so I know I must become a better listener. By listening, may I learn how to laugh and cry with the opposite sex when relationships lead us to those extremes. May I learn to value times of gentleness and friendship. May we share the love of this beautiful earth and never devalue each other because of our gender.

CHAPTER 4

IS GOD OMNIPOTENT?

Some years ago, my father, then in his middle eighties, and I were sitting on a shaded deck overlooking a beautiful inlet of the Table Rock Reservoir near Branson, Missouri. Our chaotic family vacation was underway, so there was seldom a time when he and I could talk quietly about deep things, but my father was not much given to doing that anyway.

I had a piece of family history on my mind. I knew that his little sister, Velma, had died of whooping cough at age six months in March 1926.[45] My dad was about three and a half at the time. I asked him what it was like to go through that experience at that age. He said he could remember the doctor coming to the farmhouse, staying for a few hours, and then coming out of Velma's room and telling the family that she had died. My dad remembered that his parents and older sister were in shock and angry because some older boys had gone to school with the disease and spread it to his older sister, Doris, who inadvertently gave it to

---

[45] https://www.findagrave.com/cemetery/2160491/memorial-search?firstName=velma&lastName=james&page=1#sr-14072086.

his little sister. Then I asked how his parents were affected by the experience. He said, "They certainly never went to church again." They had been attending South Persimmon Church near Sharon, Oklahoma. They had been taught that God was omnipotent and thus presumably capable of healing a baby with whooping cough.

I cannot be certain of the specific suffering Velma experienced, but the consequences of whooping cough are severe when they cause death. This includes gasping for breath, respiratory pain, and a whooping sound as the baby gasps and turns blue due to lack of oxygen. Blood vessels in the baby's face and eyes may burst, and upper airway congestion may lead to vomiting. Is this something your omnipotent god would specifically allow to happen to a baby or worse yet specifically cause it to happen? Surely not.

The Chaos of Our Lives

Family tragedies such as this often cause families to examine what they have been taught about God. If they have been taught that God is omnipotent, which is usually the case, they assume that God could have saved the life of the innocent person involved. Omnipotence for our purposes means that God can intervene into worldly happenings whenever God chooses. In my grandparents' experience, since the God they believed in had betrayed the family by allowing an innocent such as Velma to die, there was going to be no more worship and thanksgiving toward that God.

In his book *The Dishonest Church*, Rev. Jack Good tells of the family tragedy that sealed his rejection of the idea that God was omnipotent. He notes the idea that omnipotence implies that God takes the chaos out of life by being in control. This lends a level of comfort to those who cannot tolerate chaos. He notes,

> Fortunately she [his wife] and I had given up belief in an omnipotent God who oversees a neat system of just rewards and punishments when our eight-year-old grandson died mysteriously and suddenly. If we had tried to cling to a chaos-intolerant position in the face of that event, we would have lost either our faith or our minds. Or both.[46]

His view is reasonable.

Some cling to the notion that when Jesus said, "You may ask me for anything in my name, and I will do it" (John 14:15), they will get what they ask for regardless of what that might be. That is a huge misunderstanding. We want Jesus to control the worldly chaos in our lives. Here is a deeper understanding of the word *name*: "The name of someone, in the sense that the Bible authors used it, was what a person stood for, the substance of their character, or their authority."[47] Thus, the passage from John's gospel means that if you ask for anything in accordance with Jesus's nature, you will get what you really need. The writer of John elaborates that Jesus went on to say that you will receive the Counselor, the Spirit of truth, which will live with you and be in you. Jesus's nature is pure Agape Love, and this is the first

---

[46] Jack Good, *The Dishonest Church* (Scotts Valley, CA: Rising Star Press 2003), 44.

[47] Stand to Reason—Clear Thinking Christianity, https://www.str.org/articles/in-the-name-of-jesus#.XeF_duhKjIU.

fruit of Holy Spirit. A Counselor, Holy Spirit, helps us respond to the chaos of life.

Chaos is defined as a property of things in which chance is supreme or as the inherent unpredictability in the behavior of a complex natural system.[48] We live in chaos best observed when children get together in a room full of toys—a complex system. Unless one knows the children well, there is no way to predict which toys will be favored, which child will choose which toy, or the possession of which toys will lead to a fight. The implications of a chaos-tolerant view of the world are that joy and suffering fall by chance on people of good character. God is not dictating worldly events or individual actions. We have free will as committed Christians to respond to life's events.

Sometimes, raw evil perpetrated by our free will leads to unimaginable suffering. For example, in his book *Where Is God When It Hurts?* Philip Yancey retells a story originally told by Elie Wiesel. As the story goes, a boy was sentenced to death by prison guards in a Nazi concentration camp. The boy had refused to cooperate with interrogators about a cache of weapons. The boy and two men were hanged, but the boy did not die for more than half an hour because he was so light. Prisoners were forced to pass by the dead men and the struggling boy. "Where is God now?" a man asked. Wiesel said he heard an inner voice saying, "He? Here he is; He is hanging here on this gallows." Of course, the boy eventually died. Wiesel lost his faith in God in that concentration camp because he believed in an omnipotent God who could have

---

[48] https://www.merriam-webster.com/dictionary/chaos.

stopped the evil that led to the egregious death of this boy but had done nothing to prevent it.

Yancey explains why such events do not destroy his own belief in God. He notes that Jesus died an awful death on the cross. To me, Jesus's death underscores the reality that Jesus's Father was and is *not* omnipotent. A verse that sticks in my mind comes from several of the gospels (e.g., Matthew 10:38), "Whoever does not take up his cross and follow me is not worthy of me." Life will hand us crosses; God does not. Ah, but God gives us the means to carry our crosses—Holy Spirit.

A modern translation of *Night* by Elie Wiesel's sister contains a most interesting foreword by Francois Mauriac, a French Catholic.[49] Mauriac writes about his encounter with young Wiesel who had come to interview him on behalf of a Tel Aviv newspaper. Their conversation quickly reached the personal level. Wiesel shared his story from the concentration camps explaining that he had lost his belief in God when the boy was hanged. Mauriac writes that in retrospect, he explained to Wiesel that the cross of Jesus and human suffering may have helped him deal with this awful event from his youth. What Mauriac was in effect observing was that in Jesus, the idea of an omnipotent God able to save the boy Wiesel saw hanged was mistaken. Suffering is part of the chaos of our lives, and God is in how we respond to that suffering. If we respond by blaming God, we have forgotten Jesus's message.

> He who loves father or mother more than me is not worthy of me, and he who loves son or daughter more than me is not worthy of me; and he who does not

---

[49] Elie Wiesel, *Night* (New York: Hill and Wang, 2006) xxi.

take up his cross and follow me is not worthy of me.
(Matthew 10:37 RSV)

In 2010, I was in an alpha class, which was intended to be a first course on Christianity. The video lecturer was charming and probably persuaded many to believe as he did. One story he told was about his mother, who had back pain. Over a period of a few weeks, prayers spoken by her and her friends had healed her back. He took this to indicate the power of prayer. But what I know from my studies in pain and illness is that most acute back pain resolves in a few weeks without any prayers. I was unsettled by his misleading deduction, so I wrote a two-page summary called "Prayer—Another View," in which I examined the implications of misguided prayer. (In chapter 10, I will deal more in depth with prayer.) I showed my thoughts to the course leader, a young minister, and asked if I could share my view with the class. He said there was no way he was going to allow that. Since we broke into discussion groups of eight or so people after we viewed the videos, I decided to share my view in my discussion group without permission. It was well received, but a woman came to me after class asking to talk with me. She confided through tears that her daughter had been among those six students who over a two-month period in 1985 had committed suicide. Each student had attended Clear Lake High School located in a suburb of Houston. She said the worst comment she received came from a supposedly Christian friend who told her that her daughter's suicide was God's will.

This is precisely what is wrong with believing that God is omnipotent; in this case, causing or tolerating death by suicide in a young woman. God's will? Patently unreasonable unless one believes that God was exercising some loose-cannon type of wrath. I gave the woman a gentle hug knowing that there was nothing I could say to assuage her grief, which was raw even after twenty-five years. She and her daughter had been caught up in unspeakably tragic chaos.

Some young people will commit suicide; it is part of the chaos of life. One tragedy that comes to mind is the suicide of the twenty-seven-year-old son of Pastor Rick Warren, author of *The Purpose Driven Life*. The young man had a history of mental illness.[50] Any religious leader who asserts that this was God's specific will needs to consider the harm caused by preaching such beliefs. Please ask yourself if believing in an omnipotent God is reasonable. If ministry is your calling, consider preaching that God is in how we respond to the chaos that is worldly life.

▌ Lasting Bitterness

Colon cancer is the second-leading cause of cancer death in the US in men and women. About 50,000 Americans die each year from this disease. In most cases, it is unclear what caused the cancer. Several risk factors have been associated with it. These include gene mutations, sedentary lifestyle, obesity, age, race, excess alcohol consumption, and smoking.[51] Progression of the

---

[50] https://abcnews.go.com/US/pastor-rick-warrens-son-matthew-commits-suicide-lifelong/story?id=18897249.

[51] https://www.mayoclinic.org/diseases-conditions/colon-cancer/symptoms-causes/syc-20353669.

disease appears to involve formation of polyps in the rapidly reproducing lining cells of the large intestine. If left in place, these polyps may eventually form *in situ* cancer. This then invades the colon lining and may metastasize to other parts of the body including especially the liver, lung, and peritoneum (membrane lining the abdominal cavity).[52]

With that background, I wish to review a story from the book *Same Kind of Different as Me*.[53] The book is an exceptionally good read. It is both a heartwarming and heart-wrenching story of happenings in Texas a few years ago written by an evangelical Christian, Ron Hall, and his streetwise friend, Denver Moore. Ron's wife, Deborah, contracted colon cancer. First, there was the shock of diagnosis: colon cancer metastasized to the liver. Deep sadness. Then there came surgery with the tumors burned off and a promise from the surgeon that Deborah was cancer free. A Christmas present from God. But the cancer reappeared months later. More surgery on her liver. Lingering sadness that Deborah was terminal. A CT scan showed more tumors. Hospice for Deborah. Uncontrolled pain. But Deborah hung on for several more weeks until death mercifully took her. Ron captured his reaction to his wife's death, which I briefly review here.

> My fear gave way to anger, and I had plenty to go
> around. But as I fired arrows of blame—at doctors,
> the pharmaceutical industry, cancer researchers—
> clearly the bull's eye was God. It was He who had

---

[52] https://www.cancer.gov/types/metastatic-cancer.
[53] Ron Hall and Denver Moore. *Same Kind of Different as Me* (Thomas Nelson, 2006) quote from page 203. www.thomasnelson.com.

ripped a gapping and irreparable hole in my heart. Without a gun or mask, He robbed me of my wife and stole my children's mother and my grandchildren's grandmother. I had trusted Him, and He had failed me. How do you forgive that?

Having experienced my twenty-two-year-old son's unnecessary death, I know precisely how Ron felt. I wrote him a message that he should not blame God for his loss, but even then, a few years after her death, he could not accept the idea that God could not have done something to save Deborah from cancer. I am sad that Ron had been taught that God was omnipotent, and I blame those preachers that deliver this harmful message to their congregants.

▌ Thanks Be to God?

There are day-to-day consequences stemming from the notion that God is omnipotent. For years, I never questioned the idea of praying for safe travels or some other rather mundane outcome. I could rationalize that since I was never in a serious accident following such prayers, God had favored me. The reality is that about ninety people (all children of God) die each day on the roads of America. Essentially, when I pray for safe travels, I am asking God to use God's unlimited power to ensure that one of those deaths is not mine or that of my traveling companions.

Sometimes, God is thanked for safe travel to some destination once everyone arrives safely. I know Christians who have thanked God for a close parking spot at the mall or for a new Mercedes SUV. Is God so busy ensuring that we have such gifts that God neglects thousands of children that are starving each day? God's kingdom is not of this world, which means God's kingdom, where God is sovereign, assuming we hand over our free wills to God, is of the Spirit in us. A key verse in this regard is Luke 11:9–13. There, Jesus said to ask for what you wanted in the way of worldly gifts, but God would not give them to you or a nasty substitute. God would give you Holy Spirit. God's gift to all of us is Holy Spirit. Have you taken this gift?

▊ Our Free Will

Where did the idea that God is omnipotent originate? As I mentioned above, we tend to be people who do not tolerate chaos well. The biblical word for omnipotent is *sovereign*. The concordance of my NIV Study Bible lists fourteen places where God is deemed sovereign. Of these fourteen, only two appear in the New Testament. The first appears in 2 Peter 2, where the writer delivered threats to those who would challenge the sovereign Lord referring to the punishments delivered by Yahweh in stories of the Old Testament. In Jude verse 4, the writer referred to the immorality of denying Jesus Christ, our only sovereign Lord. Again, the writer reflected the power of Yahweh reported in Old Testament stories. While there is reference to stories of old when Yahweh was assumed to exert absolute worldly power, I am going to posit that this reference in Jude to a "sovereign Lord" is to our spiritual Lord Jesus, specifically, Holy Spirit as given by Jesus Christ (Jude v. 17). The notion that God is omnipotent or sovereign in worldly events simply does not add up if one clings to the belief that God is good, righteous, and just. Justice requires an even hand without favoritism.

Examined in another way, the omnipotence of God and the idea that we have free will must be in conflict. We cannot be subject to any sort of judgment if we do not have free will. If we were to suppose that God is omnipotent, our free will vanishes. C. S. Lewis declared this in his own convoluted way.[54] However, there is a way that the two may coexist if one understands God as Holy Spirit. If one is indwelled with Holy Spirit, then God does assert power over our actions, and thus we have given over a measure of our free will to God's will. Our inherent free will tends to be self-centered, but in giving over a portion of our free will to God, we overcome our selfish agendas. The best biblical example of this is the story of the Good Samaritan as told in Luke 10:25–36. Jesus discussed the law with an expert and then told him that to inherit eternal life, he had to do what was written there. The expert observed that one was to love one's neighbor as oneself. Jesus agreed, but the expert, continuing to challenge Jesus, asked, "Who is my neighbor?" (Luke 10:29 NRSV).

Jesus then told the story of a man who was robbed and beaten and left beside the road to die. First, a priest passed by keeping his distance, and a Levite did the same. But a Samaritan, despised by Jews of Jesus's time, stopped to help the man; he bandaged his wounds and took him to an inn, where he paid for the man's keep. Not only did this story call out the experts in the law of Jesus's time; it also showed someone willing to set aside his free

---

[54] C. S. Lewis on omnipotence and free will, https://www.goodreads.com/quotes/28243-his-omnipotence-means-power-to-do-all-that-is-intrinsically.

will to follow God's will. In this sense, our free will is overcome because we yield to God's will, which is to love all others as we love ourselves. Of course, we fall short again and again and again.

As I write this, mounting attention has come to the Black Lives Matter community. Much of this attention has resulted from videos of police shooting or choking to death unarmed black men. Demonstrators are gathering in large cities in the United States to collectively voice their outrage at ongoing racism. Confederate statues are being toppled in southern states. Up to a point, our free will to demonstrate is welcomed by our constitution; however, when the demonstrations become violent, authority must restrain the exercise of free will. How and when this is done is the subject of much debate. My point is that authority often constrains our free wills, but in the face of gross injustice, we may be forced to challenge authority. Jesus often challenged the Jewish leadership of his time risking his life to demonstrate righteousness and the true nature of God.

In summary, the doctrine that God is omnipotent or sovereign requires impossible assumptions. If we believe that God is always good, we cannot understand why there is so much evil, injustice, and suffering in this world. Being unwilling to give up the idea that God is always good, we must give up the idea that God is omnipotent. We must adjust our prayer life with the understanding that God lacks the power to deliver safe travel, healthy outcomes, or close parking spots. In a world of chaos, our free wills determine most outcomes.

Sometimes, favorable coincidences may seem like a God thing, but reason dictates that in a chaotic world, many chance coincidences may lead to desirable outcomes, but those are not a direct product of God's will. When we encounter those who feel betrayed by the idea of an omnipotent god, we must reassure them that God, as Holy Spirit, will be present in their responses to tragedy. Through Holy Spirit, God works for the good in all situations (Romans 8:26–27). God wills that we deliver love in the face of tragedy.

Prayer. Holy Spirit bring me to understand that together we may be co-creators of the Kingdom of God, despite the chaos of this world. As I mature in years, take my will from me, and make it your Holy will, that when the time comes for me to see my last sunset, I will do it in your presence. May I leave this world in peace, knowing that through the power and counsel of Holy Spirit I have brought God's will of love to many others. Amen

Reflection. As the years pass by, I try to do what is right, but at times I cannot fathom what that must be. There is too much chaos. I seem to lack the will to always be kind to others, so I find excuses for my failures in personal relationships. Perhaps, I must learn to discern the needs of others as I seek better relationships. Is there a force that I can lean on when my own reflections fail to make me a better person?

CHAPTER 5

YOU WERE NOT SPECIFICALLY CREATED BY GOD

▉ Right Tools

The right tool or kitchen utensil can make a difficult task much easier, but the wrong tool or utensil can bring frustration and learning. I have been on many mission trips with teenagers. One tool I keep handy is a relatively dull handsaw. We typically create wheelchair ramps sometimes reaching sixty feet long. Often, girls would refuse to use a power saw because they were afraid of the noisy, sawdust-slinging tool. So I hand them a 2 x 4 with a mark where it needed to be cut. I show them how to position it on the sawhorses, and I hold the board and watch as they break a sweat trying to saw through the board with my semi-dull handsaw. Then I ask if they would like to try the power saw using ear plugs to mitigate the noise. They often agree though I may have to steady and guide their hands through a few cuts. Soon, they are creating precisely cut boards like champs and are unwilling to give up their new skill. They have the right tool to create precise cuts that lead to excellent wheelchair ramps. The manufacturer of the power saw did not create the wheelchair ramp, and certainly that handsaw did not. The young women and their teams did.

▌ You as Cocreator

Through the process of evolution, which one may reasonably suppose God ordained from the beginning, humans have been given the capability (tools) to create new human life. I presume you do not need a description of that capability to understand it. Just like anything imbedded in the evolutionary process, those capabilities must produce imperfections to participate in evolution. Favorable imperfections will lead to an improved capability in subsequent generations whereas unfavorable imperfections will lead to less effective capability.

We have many options about how we can use our reproductive capacity, and we have expectations of creating new human beings who are at least as capable as we are. Even if we are totally responsible in using our reproductive capacity, by chance, our wishes for healthy babies might not come to pass. God's general will expressed through the mechanism of evolution is that this process will not always go as expected. Moreover, a challenging environment may dictate which humans will thrive.

The sickle cell gene is a prime example of evolutionary genetic advantages that in one environmental context confer advantage for some and in another context confer harm. Some experts discussed the situation where this genetic defect meets an environment where malaria is prevalent.[55] In a malaria-infested environment, people heterozygous (two allele variants at one location) for the gene mutation are relatively unharmed because macrophages (cellular garbage collectors) remove red cells infected with the malaria parasite. That confers an advantage. Protection does not happen for people who are homozygous (identical alleles at one location) for the genetic defect. These people suffer repeatedly in environments where malaria is present and typically do not reach an age when they can reproduce.

The process of using our capability to procreate involves much chaos; that is, it is a probabilistic activity in which one sperm cell from roughly 200 to 500 million must find and penetrate nurse cells and an ovum's cell membrane. There, the egg's cell membrane, having detected a penetrating sperm cell, goes into action to prevent further sperm cells from penetrating the membrane. The egg divides again to produce a haploid nucleus (23 chromosomes). The sperm cell (23 chromosomes) gravitates to and combines its DNA with the ovum's DNA to create the genetic foundation of a new human being with 46 chromosomes—usually but not always. Down's syndrome, for example, occurs when an extra copy of chromosome 21 is retained in the fertilized egg producing a child with trisomy 21.

Before fertilization, the ovum's chromosomes have gone partially through a complicated process called meiosis to be able to contribute half the DNA to the new, fertilized cell. Most of the million egg cells in each ovary will be lost by degeneration

---

[55] L. Luzatto, *Sickle cell anaemia and malaria* (2012) https://www.ncbi.nlm. nih.gov/pmc/articles/PMC3499995/.

by the time of puberty. Thus, the odds of a specific sperm and specific ovum forming a specific, new human being is about one in 70 trillion.[56]

After fertilization, the creative process seems even more magical. The new cell begins to divide, divide again, and divide thousands more times to gain mass. At some point, cells begin to differentiate into a variety of cell types including heart, brain, eye, and ear cells. The process is remarkable for its beauty and complexity, but it may go wrong for a variety of reasons.

Failures in Creation

God gave us wonderful procreation capability through evolution, but that capability may fail to produce a viable human, or it may produce one with serious defects. Use of bad drugs such as thalidomide early in pregnancy causes stunted limbs.[57] Exposure to the Zika virus during gestation causes microcephaly in the baby.[58] Approximately one in six recognized pregnancies will terminate in miscarriage. Approximately one in sixteen children who survives birth will have some observable genetic abnormality.[59] These often leave the child with lifelong suffering and an early death.

I know three Christian women who suffered the pain of

---

[56] "The Incredible Machine" (Washington, DC: National Geographic Society, 1986), 15–19.

[57] Thalidomide, https://www.ncbi.nlm.nih.gov/pubmed/21507989.

[58] Zika virus, https://www.cdc.gov/zika/parents/index.html.

[59] https://www.webmd.com/baby/news/20060130/top-5-genetic-birth-defects-named.

childbirth only to have their babies die minutes after delivery. The capability God gave us through evolution has failed, and our creation of a viable new human has failed. We experience deep emotional suffering. But "we know that in all things, God works for the good of those who love him and have been called according to his purpose" (Romans 8:28 NIV). God could not have forced a healthy baby to be produced, but by the power and counsel of Holy Spirit, one can find the best response to such a tragedy. Blaming God for a failed pregnancy is unreasonable just as thanking God for a healthy baby is unreasonable. God does not favor anyone, nor does God override the laws of nature to favor anyone.

Even if the baby is healthy, the new parents must continue to nurture their creation through many years of growth peppered with joy, sadness, frustration, fear, and love. I try as best I can to love others, but I have a special love for babies and children as I think most of us do. They are vulnerable and need all the love they can get.

Babies who grow up without love as part of their ongoing social creation become unstable adults.[60] Babies who are reared properly usually become responsible adults. It is in the proper rearing of children that parents nourish the spiritual, moral, physical, and intellectual abilities of their children.

In about fourteen to sixteen years, these babies become young adults capable of creating new human beings themselves because

---

[60] M. N. Christofferson et al., "The prevalence of four types of childhood maltreatment in Denmark," https://www.ncbi.nlm.nih.gov/pmc/articles/PMC3804885/.

they have developed mature capability for that undertaking. Often, the emotional and environmental constraints necessary for parents to create emotionally stable children and young adults are lacking in those unprepared to be parents. Too often, we hear on the evening news of some parent harming or killing a child. Life is not fair, and life lived as a responsible parent is not easy.

In 2001, Andrea Yates, the mother of four boys ages two to seven and a baby girl, drowned them in a bathtub.[61] This happened within a few miles of my home. Did God play and active or permissive role in this tragedy? Of course not. God is always good. Yates had a serious mental illness that her doctor and husband misunderstood.

The capability of human procreation may also be horribly misused and create unwanted children for society to manage. The most obvious example happens when a pregnancy results from rape. Rape is the stealing of sexual free will from a woman. I know of two mentally ill women who were taken advantage of by men resulting in pregnancy and childbirth. Between the women, nine children have been born; they are likely to suffer some of the same mental health problems as their birth mothers. After birth, the babies are immediately turned over to foster parents, and the misuse of reproductive capability continues.

I once talked with a couple of health care workers from West Virginia about the effects of opioid use by mothers on their newborns. They told me that I have never seen a newborn suffer like one going through opioid withdraw because the mother

---

[61] https://www.chron.com/neighborhood/article/Clear-Lake-mother-drowns-five-children-in-bathtub-9944510.php.

JOHN T. JAMES, PhD

was a user during gestation. I find it challenging to forgive such a mother, but if I make an honest attempt to understand the addictive power of drugs and genetic predisposition to addiction, I can forgive.[62] Some of my brothers and sisters are simply more vulnerable to addiction.

▌ Unscientific Beliefs

Many Christians believe that God specifically created them (knit them together in the womb), and many also believe that this was for a specific purpose in a life of ordained length (predestination). The biblical basis for these beliefs originates in Psalm 139:13–16 and Romans 8:29–30, respectively.

The writers of these passages clearly had no substantive knowledge of the cellular and molecular chaos associated with conception and subsequent embryo development in the womb. To suppose that God somehow selects one specific sperm cell from hundreds of millions to fertilize one specific ovum and does this for all conceptions including yours is unreasonable. It also disregards our free will to choose our procreation partner.

The writer of the passage from Psalms, presumably David, enjoyed a life of privilege and may have easily supposed that Yahweh favored him. Since Yahweh was the war god of Israel, one must note that in Psalm 139:21–22 (NJB), the writer declared, "Yahweh, do I not hate those who hate you, and loathe those who defy you? My hate for them has no limits, I regard them as my own enemies." This is totally incompatible with Jesus's

[62] Beth Macy, *Dopesick* (New York: Little, Brown, 2018), 122–45.

teaching about how to treat enemies. It undermines the veracity of the psalmist's idea that God is the master sperm cell and ovum selector for each of us.

Paul's belief in predestination as expressed in Romans may seem reasonable to him given his dramatic conversion and calling to spread the gospel. However, this seems to be more a product of on-the-spot divine intervention than something predestined before Paul was conceived. On the road to Damascus, Holy Spirit welled up in Paul to the point that he had to reject his previous life as a Jewish priest and persecutor of early Christians. He was called to venture out under the power of Holy Spirit to spread the good news afar (Romans 8:1–27). Paul's free will was captured by Holy Spirit at a moment in time.

The idea of predestination has other problems. First, it suggests that our free will is overridden by God's will, in which case there is no free will for us. Second, it suggests that God has arbitrarily favored some of us but not others. That is incompatible with God's justice and fairness.

There is an essential conclusion that stems from the reasonable line of thinking that we, created male and female in God's spiritual image, can in turn create our own offspring. While we do not own our creation nor does God, we are responsible for our children's welfare and have no right to abuse any child in our care. The Old Testament days of lethal punishment (Deuteronomy 21:18–21) for a disrespectful child are long past. Likewise, Father God has no role in what may seem to be punishment of us. God is fair; life is unfair. Let me give examples of unreasonable pseudo-Christian beliefs about creation.

▌ Unreasonable Beliefs

Lee Strobel wrote a series of books about Christian faith from a skeptic's point of view. He traipsed around the country to various religious scholars to get answers to his challenging questions. In my opinion, for the most part, he found reasonable Christian scholars, but at least once, he left me outraged when he interviewed Norman Geisler, then president of the Southern Evangelical Seminary in Charlotte, North Carolina.[63] The topic of discussion was the unpredictability of death especially that of children. Geisler first asserts that all are born in sin (Psalm 51). Before I thought it through, I supposed that was true. Babies are totally self-oriented and demanding, and these are hallmarks of sin in adults, but the reason babies are that way is that they must be to survive. Sin can be committed only when one is sufficiently mature to choose evil acts over righteousness.

Somehow, Geisler's misguided view of original sin points the way for God's right to take life whenever and however God chooses. This is unreasonable. Geisler asserted that during a debate, he declared that since God created life, God may take it at God's discretion. We cannot take a life because we did not create one. He claimed the audience listening to the debate applauded. Geisler also made some misbegotten analogy having to do with a person planting bushes. The one who planted the bushes in his own yard has the right to destroy them, but a neighbor does not since he does not own them.

Geisler is mistaken on several levels. He fails to appreciate the

---

[63] Lee Strobel, *The Case for Faith* (Grand Rapids, MI: Zondervan, 2000), 119.

difference between giving capabilities, say, through evolution, and creating with those capabilities. Moreover, he fails to understand that babies cannot sin, and he fails to understand that his analogy to planting bushes is irrelevant to human beings. Our reproductive capabilities are ours to create life as we see fit and are able. God has given us free will to do this. Often, these capabilities are used in loving, heterosexual relationships. From such relationships, a totally innocent, sinless baby has a good chance of being born. That baby is further created by her parents to become a responsible adult by sustained parental love. Normally, the love connection between parent and child is deeply rooted. Therefore, Geisler's analogy to ripping up plants at the will of the divine planter is nonsense. There is no mutual love between a plant and its planter. Geisler has totally sidestepped the core principle of Christianity— that we are to love all others. Jesus called specifically for little children to come to him. Geisler seems to have forgotten that Yahweh decreed that "You shall not kill" (Exodus 20:13 NJB). If we are not to kill another human being, is God holding himself to a lower standard than us by killing us like unwanted plants? Geisler's concept of God is unreasonable, and such views have caused much harm.

One example of nonsense originates from the story told by Lisa Beamer after the death of her husband in the flight that was brought down by Muslim terrorists in a field in Pennsylvania in 2001. In her book *Let's Roll*, she describes two major losses in her life.[64] The first involved her father's death due to medical errors when she was fifteen. The second was the loss of her husband

---

[64] Lisa Beamer, *Let's Roll* (Wheaton, IL: Tyndale, 2002), 82–83.

when his flight crashed in Pennsylvania due to terrorists. At the time, she was pregnant with their third child. She had asked why she had experienced such terrible losses noting that this was not fair to her. She poured out her anguish to a man from Wheaton College, a conservative Protestant institution. He consoled her about her father's death by saying that God could have changed her father's care to a better doctor or could have just healed the hole in his heart, but God did not. Lisa was conflicted about that view but was somehow set free by the viewpoint, which is consistent with Geisler's. This view is unreasonable if one is to believe in a loving, righteous, and just God whose kingdom and being is not of this world (John 17:14, 18:36).

In my opinion, a reasonable answer to Lisa's heartache would have been this: "Life is not fair; you know that Lisa. Many teenagers lose parents, and some losses will be caused by bad medical care. God's kingdom is not of this world; it is a spiritual kingdom. By chance, some people will have more worldly tragedies than others, but God is there to work for the good even in the worst tragedy. God as Holy Spirit will guide how you ultimately respond to your father's death, but you must first forgive the mistakes his doctors made in his care. Otherwise, you will continue to be angry and bitter."

It is utterly unreasonable to believe in a loving God and then accept the idea that such a god would specifically avoid saving a young father's life if that god could. Jesus would call such a god the god of the Levite and priest in the Good Samaritan story. Just walk on by.

In summary, God, through billions of years of evolution first of the universe and then of things on earth, has provided most of us with the capability to create new human beings. Biological evolution depends on alterations in DNA that may cause success or failure in succeeding generations. That was God's overarching will—a good but imperfect world. An imperfect world is essential to God's calling that we must love one another. If there were no suffering, there would be no need for love and hence no need for God. However, God never specifically ordains that a life dies in the womb, is genetically disabled, or enjoys a life free of genetic anomalies. That would be arbitrary and unjust. God is not in the business of performing physical healings though evolution has given our bodies the ability to heal in many cases through our immune systems. God has given us the power and counsel of Holy Spirit to help us through those times in life when we are overwhelmed by tragedy or loss (Romans 8:26–27). God is fair and just; life is neither.

Prayer. Father God, help me understand the bible in a way that I can use it to teach others that God is Love and that in all things, God works for the spiritual welfare of those who have suffered great loss. Help me to be gentle when communicating that God is never behind any sort of harm, and conversely, that God is not a dispenser of worldly blessings. My biological parents created me, imperfect as I am. Help me to love and respect them, always. Help me to discard old, fossilized beliefs that formed before scientific understanding of evolution was attained. Amen

Reflection. I used to think a lot about what I had understood God to be. The idea that God was somehow in control of events on earth never fit with the suffering I have seen in the world. What kind of God would allow that to happen if he could prevent it? Am I really supposed to believe that God specifically created each human being? Was I deceived by this understanding of God? Can I find a new understanding of God built on the science of evolution? Maybe, just maybe, I should start rethinking what I was taught before I decided to remain an atheist.

CHAPTER 6

GOD'S WILL AND BLESSINGS

▓ God's Will

A friend recommended that I read Leslie Weatherhead's book *The Will of God*.[65] He wrote it in the latter days of World War II from London, where the evil imposed by Nazi Germany was terrorizing, maiming, and killing many. Weatherhead's church, City Temple, was destroyed.

The edition of his venerable book I bought had a foreword by Rev. Adam Hamilton. Parts of his book are horribly time bound such as his opinion that women find self-worth only as married women with children. I also must acknowledge that he was serving a congregation that was wondering where God's will had seemed to lose authority during the desperate times of World War II. To some extent, we could likewise ask where God's will is in the current COVID-19 pandemic.

I struggled with Weatherhead's analysis of God's will in his sermons as recorded in the book because I felt that they were overly

---

[65] Leslie D. Weatherhead, *The Will of God* (Nashville: Abingdon Press, 2016).

contrived. He obliquely insists on maintaining God's omnipotence in a world filled with suffering and evil unprecedented at the time. He did this by defining three forms of God's will: intentional will, which targets only goodness for us; circumstantial will, which happens when evil forces have caused a challenge in our choices; and ultimate will, which means that God's will cannot be finally defeated. That is his definition of omnipotence.

Quite often, Weatherhead brushes remarkably close to my belief that God works through our responses to circumstances generated in a world full of chaos and evil. He notes that we may become "instruments of God's purpose" (p. 13), "The circumstances of evil have often been an occasion for the expression of good" (p. 16), "The second part of God's circumstantial will cannot be done without human cooperation" (p. 29), and "There is the possibility of the [diseased] patient making such a splendid response to that circumstance that he creates out of it a spiritual asset" (p. 35). In reference to an unmarried woman, he asserts that God's ultimate will is "to make her a complete and integrated personality in union with himself" (p. 29). Obviously, this often does not happen in our world where suicide, addiction, and childhood deaths claim many lives that were never integrated in union with God. Such people never fully become children of God.

Weatherhead clearly recognizes humanity's free will and acknowledges that God is Love (p. 40), but he rarely mentions Holy Spirit. His opinion of germs that cause disease leads him to question why God created them but supposes that in the evolutionary process, they serve some good purpose. In my opinion, it is much less contrived to simply acknowledge that

Holy Spirit is God in us impelling us to be agents of his will on earth. God wills that we love one another. Love must be our response to terrible times.

Many in the caregiver professions are being asked to heal those who are ill from the pandemic with extraordinary courage and perseverance. Their response is God's will. Others have responded to our pandemic by asserting that it is their right to gather in huge groups with no masks for protection of themselves or others. I believe this is contrary to God's will.

Praise God for What?

One activity that troubles me in my church unfolds when the money collection is brought forward to be presented to the presiding minister. At that point, we are supposed to sing, "Praise God from whom all blessing flow." I do not sing. The implication is that the money we possess is somehow a blessing flowing from God. It is our Christian duty to give back a portion—10 percent is sometimes suggested—of what God has given us. Since God has favored us with worldly blessings, we are expected to return the favor by giving to God's church.

The problem with this view is twofold. First, God's kingdom is spiritual, not worldly. While the two worlds are connected through our senses, desires, and actions, they are distinct. That might not set well with some congregations, but it is the truth that Jesus brought to us (John 18:36; 1 John 2:15). The apostle John further warned of the dangers of worldly stuff.

> Do not love the world or anything in the world. If anyone loves the world, the love of the Father is not in him … The world and its desires pass away, but those who do the will of God live forever. (1 John 2:15, 17 NRSV)

This brings to my mind the prayer many of us repeat every Sunday, but I suspect often without our hearts and minds fully engaged. It is the Lord's Prayer. The second phrase of that great prayer is, "Thy Kingdom come, thy will be done on earth as it is in heaven." Have you ever asked yourself how God's will shall be done on earth? That question is answered in the above passages from the book of John: "Those who do the will of God live forever." "Those" is you and me. I would amend the Lord's Prayer with the statement "Thy kingdom come, thy will be done on earth *by us* as it is in heaven." We are the conduit of God's will while on earth. We are to be God's blessing to others perhaps by answering their prayers.

Second, God's greatest gift to all of us is Holy Spirit. Even those who are the poorest of the poor may be blessed by Holy Spirit. The richest of the rich may be impelled by Holy Spirit to give huge sums to help those who suffer rather than buy a 123-foot yacht or another mansion in some exotic location. And this is not because God has blessed them with riches; it is because their hearts have been made radically generous. They have seen the eyes of Jesus in those who suffer (Matthew 25:31–46).

Unfortunately, the generosity of the rich is rare. As the Bible properly warns with the words ascribed to Jesus as the Pharisees listened,

> No servant can serve two masters. Either he will hate the one and love the other, or he will be devoted to one and despise the other. You cannot serve both God and mammon. (Luke 16:13 RSV)

▦ Are You One of God's Favorites?

I have known many Christians who suppose God has favored them in worldly ways. They do realize that many have not been as fortunate as they have, but they fail to see that God does not play favorites (Acts 10:34; Romans 2:11; James 2:1). Peter said in Acts "that God has no favorites, but that anybody of any nationality who fears him and does what is right is acceptable to him" (NJB). Paul wrote in Romans, "There will be glory and honor and peace for everyone who does good, the Jew first and also the Greek. For God shows no partiality" (NRSV). James warned, "My brothers and sisters, do you with your acts of favoritism really believe in our glorious Lord Jesus Christ?" (NRSV).

The so-called prosperity gospel is one of the great fabrications of counterfeit Christianity.[66] Christian professor David W. Jones outlines errors with the prosperity gospel.[67]

1. The Abrahamic covenant is a means to material entitlement.
2. Jesus's atonement extends to the "sin" of material poverty.

---

[66] https://en.wikipedia.org/wiki/Prosperity_theology.

[67] David W. Jones, https://www.thegospelcoalition.org/article/5-errors-of-the-prosperity-gospel/.

3. Christians give in order to gain material compensation from God.

4. Faith is a self-generated spiritual force that leads to prosperity.

5. Prayer is a tool to force God to grant prosperity.

Pastor John Piper in 2014 expounded six ways to detect prosperity gospel.[68]

1. The absence of a doctrine of the normalcy of suffering
2. The absence of a prominent doctrine of self-denial
3. The absence of serious analysis of scripture
4. The absence of dealing with tensions in scripture
5. Church leaders who live exorbitant lifestyles
6. Focus on self rather than on God

I recall a U.M. (United Methodist) Army T-shirt from a few years ago that was worn by youth doing mission work for poor Texans who were desperate for help with a wheelchair ramp, a leaky roof, or a crumbling home. That shirt declared, "It's not about me." Several of the youth came back transformed in their beliefs.

The counterfeit nature of the prosperity gospel in any form must be spoken against because unfortunately, it sells well to people who accept what a preacher says as truth. John Wesley, the founder of Methodism, had this view of money: "Having, First, gained all you can [without sacrificing health or life], and,

---

[68] Detecting prosperity gospel: https://www.desiringgod.org/interviews/six-keys-to-detecting-the-prosperity-gospel

Secondly saved all you can, Then 'give all you can."[69] Note first of all that it is you who gains (earns) money; it's not God giving you money. Wesley was often preaching to people who lived on the edge of starvation, so the second stipulation points to the need to be ready to survive hard times. The third stipulation points to the expectation of God that we give generously. There is no suggestion that God will provide money or prosperity.

▉ Trivial Favors

Some Christians I know and respect as quite reasonable and intelligent have troubled me with their belief in God things. They seem to assume that God is omnipotent as I described in chapter 4. The reasoning in that chapter is worth repeating here. I have heard such people thank God for a close parking space at the mall or airport, I have heard God thanked for a green traffic light when in a hurry, I have heard God thanked for safe travel over a long distance, and I have heard God thanked for giving someone a new Mercedes SUV. Personifying God for the moment, how would you feel if someone you loved was constantly thanking you for things you never did? At best, I would feel odd and troubled by the misperception of that person.

If your God finds parking spots for you, manages traffic lights, and ensures your safe travel, please rethink what you believe. Many helpless children are starving, war is destroying the lives of thousands of innocent people, 30,000 Americans die each year

[69] John Wesley on use of money: https://www.unitedchurchofsoro.org/john-wesleys-sermon-50-on-the-use-of-money/

in vehicle accidents, and God is busy doing these special favors for you. Really? Why would God favor you by manipulating worldly events? Such a belief seems unreasonable, and it flies in the face of God being understood as just and loving except on the spiritual level.

Miracles?

Miracles as most stringently defined are events that happen to an individual or small group of people requiring God to set aside the physical and biological laws (evolution) that God created to govern the world and the creatures that occupy it. As our understanding of physics and biology has matured since the days of Jesus, we have come to understand that events that were once perceived as miracles were nothing more than the application of physical or biological laws not understood at the time.

One of my favorite miracle stories involves an ancient stone Madonna statue that wept at certain times of the day and year. It was clear to onlookers that tears were emerging from near the top of the statue and flowing down across the Madonna's face and stone robe. At the time, no one understood that the cold surface of the statue was condensing water vapor from the warm, humid air and forming drops that flowed down the statue. It was no miracle. Jesus warned, "False Christs and false prophets will appear and perform signs and miracles to deceive the elect—if that were possible. So, be on your guard" (Mark 13:22–23 NIV). Let us search for real miracles if such may be found.

▓ Biological Miracles

Miracles of healing abound in the New Testament. Although many claim miracles continue to occur, others posit that the age of miracles ended with the apostolic age.

There are three types of miracle healing to be considered: returns from the dead, physical healings in the face of long odds, and emotional healings from mental illnesses. Returns from the dead may often be explained by understanding that doctors even today may not always know when someone is fully dead.[70] Healings of physical illness may often be explained by the actions of our immune systems to overcome infections or even cancer. In fact, many effective cancer treatments now depend on enhancing cancer patients' immune systems.[71] Mental health healings may often be explained by the placebo effect. It is well known that those who think they are taking a pill to cure depression may actually experience relief from depression even though the pill is inert.[72] I'd suggest that an emotional or religious healing experience does the same thing to the brain freeing the person from the demon of depression. These are not miracles. Let us continue our search.

---

[70] Carla Valentine, "Why waking up in a morgue is not quite as unusual as you think," *The Guardian*, https://www.theguardian.com/commentisfree/2014/nov/14/waking-morgue-death-janina-kolkiewicz.

[71] "NCI's Role in Immunotherapy," https://www.cancer.gov/research/key-initiatives/immunotherapy.

[72] https://www.nih.gov/news-events/nih-research-matters/placebo-effect-depression-treatment.

▌ Miracles of Holy Spirit

One of my favorite hymns is "Amazing Grace." John Newton wrote this most recognized of all Christian hymns. As the story goes,[73] he was an untrustworthy and profane man in the slave trading business. During a voyage in 1748, a violent storm hit his ship, and he furiously pumped water and steered the *Greyhound* for many hours through rough seas to safety. Gradually, after surviving this seminal event and spending more years in the slave trade, he was brought to humility that started him on his road to becoming a committed Christian.

Newton was encouraged by John Wesley, the founder of Methodism, to enter the clergy. He wrote the lyrics to "Amazing Grace" in 1772 and published it in 1779. Who can forget the opening words? "Amazing grace, how sweet the sound that saved a wretch like me. I once was lost, but now am found; was blind but now I see." Newton's salvation was the patient work of Holy Spirit (God's grace) entering his unsettled heart. Indeed, a spiritual miracle.

To reinforce this perspective, I want to review another definition of miracles. Philosopher Richard L. Purtill posited that

> A miracle is an event that is brought about by the power of God that is a temporary exception to the ordinary course of nature for the purpose of showing that God is acting in history.[74]

---

[73] https://en.wikipedia.org/wiki/Amazing_Grace.
[74] Lee Strobel, *The Case for Miracles* (Grand Rapids, MI: Zondervan, 2018), 49.

This definition falls short by not explicitly considering the power of Holy Spirit, yet I see truth in it. As we may glean from the New Testament, the power of Holy Spirit *does* enable us to overcome our natural limitations and fears thus making a miraculous mark in history. Jesus told his disciples,

> The Counselor, the Holy Spirit, whom the Father will send in my name, will teach you all things and will remind you of everything I have said to you. Peace, I leave with you; my peace I give you. I do not give you as the world gives. Do not let your hearts be troubled and do not be afraid. (John 14:26–27 NIV)

The story of Dietrich Bonhoeffer is a well-known example of a miracle of the Spirit. He returned to Germany from the US in the days when his death was likely upon his return. There is no stronger natural force in humans than self-preservation to thwart death, yet Bonhoeffer faced likely death at the hands of Hitler's henchmen as he served in the German resistance. He was imprisoned for one and a half years and hanged in April 1945 after being sentenced to death by an SS judge.[75] I would opine that under Purtill's definition of miracle, Bonhoeffer's choice to leave the security of the US and return to his native Germany despite the personal risk was a miracle wrought by Holy Spirit.

Jesus's feeding of the multitudes is a story often repeated in the New Testament. One of my favorite commentators on the Bible is William Barclay. What I like about his comments on passages is that he typically presents several possibilities for understanding it. Here, I want to present one of his views on a time when Jesus

---

[75] https://en.wikipedia.org/wiki/Dietrich_Bonhoeffer.

fed 5,000 men (John 6:1–13). As Barclay notes, one may interpret the passage as a physical miracle that five loaves and two fish were able to feed so many people. Given that interpretation, I have sometimes wondered how the miracle unfolded. Was the crowd suddenly not hungry? Were fish and bread miraculously appearing in the basket as it was passed? Then I encountered Barclay's alternate interpretation which he called a "lovely explanation."

> It is scarcely to be thought that the crowd left on a 9-mile expedition without making any preparations at all. If there were pilgrims with them, they would certainly possess supplies for the way. But it may be that none would produce what he had, for he selfishly—and very humanly—wished to keep it all for himself … Moved by his [Jesus's] example, everyone who had anything did the same [shared]; and in the end there was enough, and more than enough for all.[76]

In my opinion, this was a story of Holy Spirit as the Spirit of Jesus working through the crowd that had trusted and followed him—a miracle by Purtill's definition.

There are fundamental problems with the belief in worldly miracles as events in which the creator God sets aside the laws of nature to benefit someone. Typically, such miracles are often described in terms of miraculous healings. I remember when I was a kid watching a profusely sweating, prosperity-gospel preacher named Oral Roberts on a black-and-white TV perform what appeared to be miracle healings on folks at one of his revivals.

---

[76] William Barclay, *The Gospel of John*, volume 1 (Louisville: Westminster John Knox Press, 1975), 204.

If these were true miracles, we must admit that God is arbitrary and unjust. Arbitrary because God often does not deliver miracles when prayers beg for healing. My son's death and Lisa Beamer's father's death from bad medical care are examples of nonmiracles. If miracles happen according to the stringent definition, God is also unjust. Justice requires an even hand with divine mercy. However, and this is the crux of my argument, understanding spiritual miracles as emanating from the power of Holy Spirit is neither arbitrary nor unjust. It is available to all, and it passes the test of reasonability.

In summary, we Christians must be wary of thanking God for worldly favors. Whether these are trivial favors such as green lights, success at the casino, or safe travel, they are not from God. Miracles of unexplained healing and grand prosperity do not emanate from God on an individual basis. Through Creator-ordained evolution, our bodies have developed amazing ways to heal either through our immune systems or through the power of a positive mindset (the placebo effect). In a world of chaos, some will become wealthy, and others will live out their short lives in desperate poverty.

If you think God has specifically favored you with wealth or health, you are mistaken. Your God is unjust and arbitrary. If you acknowledge that Holy Spirit has impelled you to share in the suffering of others and act with radical love, you are running the race asked of true believers. If you do not wish to acknowledge Holy Spirit as an agent in your life, at least live your secular life for the good of those who suffer. Your reward in this life will be great.

Prayer. Holy Spirit of Jesus, open my eyes to the needs of others, that I may not focus my faith on my own needs. Help me to honor your legacy by knowing that your kingdom is one of Holy Spirit and not of materialism or worldly favor. May I always know that God's will on earth is to be done by us. Help me to be an answer to the prayers of others, especially those who suffer from hunger, war, and oppression. Help me to exhibit fruits of Holy Spirit in all I do, that I may find peace in the face of injustice, suffering and death. Amen

Reflection. I must find better ways to live my life. Perhaps I must go with less self-centered drive and intensity, so that I can make time to recognize in others the need for companionship. I must find more time to listen to the stories of others, focusing less on my story and my needs. No matter how different someone may be from me, I will make time to listen to their story and respond with patience and kindness. Perhaps I may become a 'miracle' worker.

CHAPTER 7

FEAR NOT

▓ History of Fear in the Church

One of my favorite books about Christianity is *The Faith—A History of Christianity* by Brian Moynahan, a Cambridge-educated historian and news correspondent. I came across half a dozen copies of the 800-page tome in a used bookstore and bought all six. Later, I used these to teach high schoolers in Sunday school about the history of the church to which they belonged.

I enjoy the way Moynahan traces the progress of the church with secular reactions to the so-called progress. Among the many happenings he captures are two that embodied the heavy-handed use of Christian fear.

In the mid-twelfth century, the need arose to unmask heretics, those who did not see Christian beliefs as dictated by the leadership of the Roman Catholic Church. Inquisitions were born. Among the earliest targets were the Cathars, who were living in southern France and northern Italy.[77] They believed that the material world was an evil creation and that one's body was a prison for the soul. The Catholic Church was part of that evil. The world of spirit was the creation of a good God who through Jesus showed us the Spirit as the means of salvation.

One source opines that the Cathars saw the evil God as represented by the God of the Old Testament and the good God by the New Testament.[78] This is a reminder of the first Christian canon due to Marcion about 150 CE. For the Cathars, Jesus was viewed as a phantom. The Cathars' only sacrament was laying on of hands to impart Holy Spirit upon believers. Their leaders lived austere lives much in contrast to the wealthy leaders of the Roman Catholic Church.

During the campaign against the Cathars, eyes were gouged out and noses cut off. Hundreds were burned alive. According to Moynahan, the pope at the time took joy in learning of this approach to dealing with heretics. For their part, the Cathars were boldly critical of the orthodox church and its sacraments and labeled it "the whore of Babylon." In fear, the surviving Cathars pretended to go along with Catholic rituals. The Cathars had been annihilated by the early fourteenth century.

In a second tale of fear, Moynahan describes witch hunts in disturbing terms.[79] These were conducted in Europe beginning

[77] Brian Moynahan, *The Faith—A History of Christianity* (New York: Doubleday, 2002), 277–85.

[78] https://en.wikipedia.org/wiki/Catharism.

[79] Brian Moynahan, *The Faith—A History of Christianity* (New York: Doubleday, 2002), 479–85.

in 1484 and ended in 1692 after crossing the Atlantic to New England. The basis of this stain was the church both Catholic and Protestant following a passage from Exodus 22:18 (NJB): "You shall not allow a sorceress to live." The deaths included men and children as well as women. Some of the tortures turn one's stomach. A person might have his hands tied behind his back, weights attached to his legs, and his body hoisted aloft, and then he was dropped to dislocate his shoulders. In the face of such punishment, the witch would have to name other witches, so there was an unending supply of victims. It is estimated that more than 100,000 supposed witches were hanged, drowned, or burned alive in Europe. Clearly, when authorities, often bishops, came searching for witches, there was great fear. One did not challenge the dictates of the church.

Facing Fear with Courage

The earthly tortures of centuries ago no longer exist in modern Christian practice; however, vestiges of fear and courageous responses remain. In the late 1990s, my family entertained a Russian contingent with whom we were partnered to manage air quality during the Shuttle-Mir space program. It was a joyful evening at my house. I had purchased cognac for the occasion. At one point, my counterpart, a seventy-year-old Russian toxicologist named Valentine Savina, began chasing my young son around the house with a huge red rocket the boy had made. They were giggling with delight even though neither could speak a word of the other's language.

We had been warned by our interpreter to stay away from

politics and religion, but I had harbored a burning question since my first visit to Russia in 1994, and I risked asking it. Noting the concerted, multigenerational purges of the Russian Orthodox Church by Stalin and the sudden massive recovery of the church in the 1990s after decades of apparent absence, I asked Dr. Savina where the church had hidden during Stalin's purges. She smiled showing her collection of gold teeth and through our interpreter said, "At grandma's house." I realized that the use of political fear from outside the church had actually strengthened it as an underground ember ready to reignite the Russian Orthodox Church when the awful purges ceased.

Unfortunately, ingrown fear still prevails in many church traditions. This takes the form of belief in eternal punishment for those not subscribing to church doctrine. For example, the Southern Baptists in 2011 asserted as follows.

> RESOLVED, That the messengers to the Southern Baptist Convention, meeting in Phoenix, Arizona, June 14–15, 2011, do hereby affirm our belief in the biblical teaching on eternal, conscious punishment of the unregenerate in Hell; and be it finally RESOLVED, That out of our love for Christ and for His glory, and our love for lost people and our deep desire that they not suffer eternally in Hell, we implore Southern Baptists to proclaim faithfully the depth and gravity of sin against a holy God, the reality of Hell, and the salvation of sinners by God's grace alone, through faith alone, in Jesus Christ alone, to the glory of God alone.[80]

---

[80] SBC reality of hell: https://www.baptistpress.com/resource-library/sbc-life-articles/hell-the-place-of-everlasting-punishment/

Writing near the end of his life, Billy Graham asserted,

> I can say with certainty that if there is no literal fire in
> Hell, then God is using symbolic language to indicate
> something far worse. Just as there are no words to
> adequately describe the grand beauty of Heaven, we
> cannot begin to imagine just how horrible the place
> called Hell is.[81]

This seems to me to be fearmongering. It is much more reasonable to recruit new church members because of the way God loves us by being Love rather than by the threat of eternal punishment after death. Please ask yourself if your fear of hell is impelling you to be a Christian. I do not think you want to evangelize using this threat.

Pope Francis, whom I highly respect, has a different view of hell. "This is hell," he said.

> It is telling God, "You take care of yourself because
> I'll take care of myself." They don't send you to hell,
> you go there because you choose to be there. Hell is
> wanting to be distant from God because I do not want
> God's love. This is hell.[82]

This view, which is shared by many Christians I know, is reasonably consistent with what Methodists believe. Formally, there may be a hell of some sort, but to preach based on the fear of hell is simply unreasonable to me. I've heard hundreds of sermons

[81] Billy Graham on reality of Hell: https://www.cnsnews.com/blog/michael-w-chapman/billy-graham-when-unsaved-sinner-dies-they-go-hell
[82] https://www.ncronline.org/news/opinion/signs-times/pope-francis-and-hell.

by Methodist preachers, and not once have I heard that we should believe because we fear hell. I cannot say that is so for the few Baptist sermons I have experienced.

Fear God?

If you ask your minister what it means to fear God in the biblical sense, he or she is likely to reply with phrases such as "have reverence for God" or "have respect for God." Sometimes, this fear gets strangely married to positive outcomes depending on how one views such outcomes. For example, a writer of *Christian Bible Studies* warns as follows: "Don't be afraid of those who want to kill your body; they cannot touch your soul. Fear only God, who can destroy both soul and body in hell (Matthew 10:28)." This declaration is supposedly a positive application of fear.[83] This is a clear statement that we should fear God more than we should fear someone who could murder us. One must not fear an ordinary killer-dragon more than one that breathes the fire of hell. Fear in the Bible means fear.

To understand why "fear God" in the Bible means just that, one must use a concordance Bible to find words that characterize behavior ascribed to God mostly but not exclusively in the Old Testament. These include the words *anger, curse, destroyed, hell, judgment, terror,* and *wrath*. A deity with these alleged powers and attributes is certainly one that should be feared. Even the Ten Commandments contain a strong element of fear. In Exodus

---

[83] https://www.christianitytoday.com/biblestudies/bible-answers/spirituallife/what-does-it-mean-to-fear-god.html.

20:4–6, we read that we must never make an idol for ourselves to worship. That seems reasonable. But then the assertion is backed up by the threat that if we break this commandment, God, being the jealous sort, will punish our children to the third and fourth generations.

The New Testament is far from free of threats of hell. In an example of the hyperbole of some of Jesus's sayings (Matthew 5:29–31), he is supposed to have warned that if your eye or your hand causes you to sin, you are to gouge out your eye or amputate your hand. The reason for this is that losing one part of your body would be better than your whole body going to hell. In Mark 9:45–46, another body part, the foot, is added to potential sinful parts that must be amputated if it causes sin. In a bold attack on the teachers of the law and the Pharisees, Jesus warned them that they would be condemned to hell because they bore the sin of their forefathers, which was shedding the blood of the prophets (Matthew 23:33). Fear is a strong motivator. I am sad that it remains in some modern Christian traditions.

An interesting, fear-based reason for believing originated from philosopher Blasé Pascal (1623–1662). He began by asserting that one could neither prove nor disprove the existence of the theistic God. In the face of this uncertainty, one must choose to believe or not to believe. In its simplest terms, the argument goes as follows:[84] If one wagers on God existing but there is no God, nothing has been lost. If one wagers on God and God exists, one wins eternity in heaven. If one wagers against God and there is a God as described in the Bible, this life will be followed by a

---

[84] https://plato.stanford.edu/entries/pascal-wager/#ArguGeneExpePascWage.

long period of misery (hell). If one wagers against God and there is no God, nothing is lost or gained. This argument embodies fundamental misunderstandings about God the most glaring of which is that one does not gain heaven by intellectually wagering on God's existence. The truth is that the truly committed Christian sacrifices his or her life for the kingdom of God to be built up on earth. Of course there is the dark cloud of fear reminding one to bet on God because a bet that there is no God could mean an endless period in hell. Pascal's original writings on this subject were confusing, but this has not stopped theologians and philosophers from cooking various lines of analysis until any abiding truth has been burned to char in an intellectual Hades (my opinion).

In conclusion, the last word on fear comes from John's first letter (4:16–18 NRSV).

> God is love, and those who abide in love abide in God and God abides in them … There is no fear in love, but perfect love casts out fear, for fear has to do with punishment, and whoever fears has not reached perfection in love.

If you are a Christian because you are afraid of God's wrath and punishment in this life or an afterlife, you have taken a wrong turn. Go the other direction. Practice love every waking moment of every day. Fear of God will have no place in your life or beliefs.

Prayer. I must admit that sometimes I fear placing my beliefs on the line when I unveil them to others. Just as Jesus told his disciples to follow Holy Spirit in the face of daunting odds, help me have the courage to witness my faith to all who might listen. Help me to listen before I witness, that I may be a worthy evangelist. Help me to never use fear as a selling point for Christianity. Amen

Reflection. I can look back on my life and see times when I feared doing the right thing. Maybe I ignored someone who needed a ride, or a beggar at a stop light, or an old person lost in confusion. I want to be fearless in the face of others in need. Especially, I want to be fearless in the face of injustice, even to the point of risking my life and wellbeing to thwart injustice. Where might I find the power and wisdom to accomplish this? How might I become fearless?

CHAPTER 8

THE POWER OF HOLY SPIRIT

As I noted in the prologue, I can trace my religious upheaval to a single, seminal experience that happened just as I was grieving the loss of my son, who had died a few months earlier. I was reading Romans 8 as I sat on a bench facing the back of his grave marker. It seemed that the small New Testament I had brought opened to this chapter on its own. As I read, I felt the indwelling of Holy Spirit as strongly as if I had been struck by a large-caliber bullet. Other people I know have had a sudden Holy Spirit experience that changed their lives. Others have experienced Holy Spirit as whispers in a small voice that gradually beckons the Spirit to be welcomed into one's heart. Holy Spirit is God in us, conforming us to God's will and to the example God gave us in human form—Jesus. Holy Spirit impels us to agape on steroids. Although Christian tradition imagines that Holy Spirit is male, I will not follow that tradition because I know that God has no gender and therefore Holy Spirit can have no gender.

▌ A Personal Story of Holy Spirit

I am not a fan of speaking in tongues as an outward expression of Holy Spirit. Based on the early verses of 1 Corinthians 13, Paul was not either. He subordinated speaking in tongues as a direct communication to God because no one could understand those who spoke in tongues. Paul much preferred prophesy, writing earlier that those tongues would be stilled but (agape) love would never fail.

Despite my reservations about speaking in tongues, a highly educated woman I know recalls a seminal Holy Spirit experience that turned her life around. It involved speaking in tongues (gibberish). Below is her story in her own words.

> I had been attending Alcoholics Anonymous (AA) meetings for 18 months resulting in varying periods of sobriety, but I always felt I was going to return to drinking alcohol. And I did. Then someone told me about Power in Praise by Merlin Carothers. It seemed a bit over wrought for my sophisticated religious tastes, but I was desperate. These are Carothers' words: "The lady told me I could speak with tongues if I just opened my mouth and let the language come out. I hesitated and thought that now I was really making a fool of myself. . . I did notice some strange "words" forming in my mind, and I opened my mouth and said them out loud. They sounded silly, and my instant reaction was to think, "You're faking it Merlin; you're just making up a bunch of gibberish." (page 54), and on page 56, "When we speak in tongues, we communicate directly from our spirit to God ... and we bypass the control-centers of our critical understanding.

I felt impelled to try Carothers' pathway. It was foolishness, but somehow, it bypassed my sensible objections to it and overwhelmed me. It was an ordinary weekday, and I was doing something in the kitchen. Without thinking, I fell to my knees as Carothers had suggested and spoke "gibberish." Carothers didn't register much change until somewhat later, but I felt an immediate effect. I can't fully describe my experience with words. It was not a flash of light, but a sensation similar to the sun suddenly breaking through after a rain shower. It only lasted a moment, and was slightly alarming, but I got up from my knees and I immediately knew that I never would have another drink. It was as though a physical weight had been lifted from my heart. And I haven't had a drink since that day in August of 1974. It was the most remarkable experience of my life - I never had another craving for a drink. I had found that deciding not to drink and managing this with my own resources was a recipe for misery and eventual relapse. I attended AA meetings for the next twenty-five years which moved me a little closer to the sane marking on the mental health dial. AA's Big Book says: "Drinking is but a symptom of our problem." In that book, Carl Jung is quoted roughly as follows: for an alcoholic to cease drinking, there must be a spiritual awakening. True.

I have never tried speaking in tongues again. It was so contrary to my supposedly rational, over-educated mentality. It was the stuff of hillbillies and holy rollers. Maybe it was, but it sure as [Hades] worked for me. Maybe I'm afraid of where the Spirit might lead me if I stayed "open" to it. I suppose you could say I opened up in desperation, and once the Spirit saved my [back end], I put it back in its box and didn't have the courage to let it out again. Why did the Spirit come to me then? The Big Book (our Bible) of AA says, "Some of us tried to hold onto our old ideas, and the result was nil until we let go absolutely," and letting go absolutely is the hardest thing to ask any person to do. By God's grace, I was able to put aside my ego long enough to allow Holy Spirit to enter me with full force and to do for me what I could not do for myself. With Holy Spirit, once was enough.

Others whom I respect have cautioned me against being too critical of speaking in tongues. This may be viewed as a process that clears one's mind of worldly thinking and self-centered concerns. I would opine that if speaking in tongues leads one to deeper truths centered on agape love, repentance, and the casting aside of sin, then it is a legitimate form of communication with God. It must lead to a message from God that impels the speaker to see suffering in others and act with power and courage to love them, just as God has willed us to do. If it results in the same feeling one gets at a rock concert—euphoria of the moment— then speaking in tongues is not legitimate Christian witness.

▓ Third-String God

Without Holy Spirit, there would be no Christian Church. There is little doubt that these days, Holy Spirit is the *Forgotten God* as reflected in Francis Chan's 2009 book with that title. He is right about Holy Spirit being forgotten. Except for preaching near the time modern Christians acknowledge Pentecost, Holy Spirit is seldom the focus of any preaching. In my opinion, Jesus's gift of

Holy Spirit ranks equal to the gift of forgiveness of sins he brought to humankind during his presence on earth.

Sadly, this great gift was for centuries the focus of controversy between the Eastern and Western Christian churches and split the Christian world in two. The issue came to a head in the great schism of 1054. In this year, the patriarch of Constantinople, leader of the Eastern Church, and the pope who led the Western Church, excommunicated each other. The issue was whether Holy Spirit proceeded from the Father only (Eastern view) or from the Father *and* the Son (Western view). There were other reasons for the schism including papal celibacy and the use of unleavened bread, but all this seems incredibly silly to me. Except for the end of the gospel of Matthew, the Trinity is not even implicitly suggested anywhere in the Bible. Fortunately, after 911 years of separation, in 1965, the leaders of the Eastern and Western Churches revoked their excommunications. I would argue that it was Holy Spirit that healed this great schism of the Christian Church.

To further reinforce my view that Holy Spirit is too often overlooked in substantive Christian writing, I will point to a book by Jimmy Carter, a devout Southern Baptist and former president who has written several books on faith. In his most recent book, *Faith a Journey for All*, he mentions Holy Spirit only once.[85] He declares, "In his crucifixion, Jesus has taken our punishment, and through repenting and accepting this forgiveness we are reconciled with God and can now have eternal life, with Holy

---

[85] Jimmy Carter, *Faith a Journey for All* (New York: Simon and Schuster, 2018), 98.

Spirit dwelling within us." This deep insight caused me to wish that President Carter would have written more about his sense of Holy Spirit. At age ninety-five, he is still responding to the will of God by lovingly working with Habitat for Humanity for those who cannot afford houses.[86] Is this not the will of God, which we must all do?

Holy Spirit Misunderstood

I might begin to characterize Holy Spirit by what it is not. A prime example of misunderstandings are the views expressed by Francis Chan in *Forgotten God*. Of course, these are mixed with many valid understandings. Unfortunately, he seems to be wedded to the belief that the understanding of God in the Old and New Testaments are synonymous; that distorts his understanding. It's hardly a secret that I am not a fan of many of the tenets of orthodoxy, which Chan believes must constrain our construct of Holy Spirit. I believe that is the root of our differences. I must point out that while I am critical of Chan's view of Holy Spirit, his view is embraced by many, and so I am being critical of many Christians who may disagree with my experience of Holy Spirit.

It is asserted that actions of Holy Spirit may be traced through the Old Testament. According to my concordance, there are only two places in the Old Testament where Holy Spirit is named apart from the "Spirit of God," Psalm 51:11 and Isaiah 63:10. In the first, David cried out to Yahweh not to take Yahweh's spirit of

---

[86] https://thehill.com/blogs/in-the-know/in-the-know/464705-jimmy-carter-back-to-building-homes-for-habitat-for-humanity.

holiness (NJB; translated "Holy Spirit" in the NIV) from him as the result of his infidelity with Bathsheba. The second mention is also interesting. In my NJB, the passage is this.

> But they [Israelites] rebelled and vexed his [Yahweh's] holy Spirit. Then he became their enemy and himself waged war on them ... But he called the past to mind, Moses his servant ... Where was he who put his holy Spirit among them, whose glorious arm led the way by Moses' right hand.

My NIV Bible has essentially the same translation, but in that rendering, "holy" is written as "Holy." I'm thinking that those who prepared the NJB did not feel that Holy Spirit given by Jesus was in fact present in the days of David and Isaiah whereas those who wrote the NIV translation had a different view. I go with the former.

For me, one of the great misunderstandings of Holy Spirit is that it is not of God. This view is reflected in the Jehovah's Witnesses who occasionally visit us with their Watchtower booklets. Their Bible, the New World Translation, is in many ways like the New Jerusalem Bible used by the Catholics. The former typically calls Old Testament God "Jehovah" and the latter calls God "Yahweh" when reference is made to the same stories or specific psalms.

In the New Testament, the two diverge. In the New Jerusalem Bible, Holy Spirit is capitalized indicating divine nature and name. In the New World Translation, it is never capitalized. For example, in Matthew 1:18 (NWT), we read, "But the birth of Jesus Christ was in this way. During the time his mother Mary was promised in marriage to Joseph, she was found to be pregnant by holy spirit before they were united." Upon investigation of this difference, my eyes were opened. While the Jehovah's Witnesses do not recognize holy spirit as part of a triune God, they assert that holy spirit is a divine force but not a person.[87] The more orthodox view is that our God is one in three persons—Father, Son, and Holy Spirit. But the orthodox thinkers must admit that the Trinity is not clearly biblical. The doctrine of Trinity was fully developed only at the end of the fourth century.[88] My personal experience with Holy Spirit, which I take to be fully one with God, is that it is not a person; it is God in us to empower us to do God's will.

The idea that Holy Spirit is somehow a person is mistaken. Holy Spirit is characterized in the New Testament as a flame or wind (Acts 2:1–5; John 3:7–10). While we may try to personify these facets of nature (e.g., naming hurricanes), we know that such things are not persons. Holy Spirit is like a flame because once the light of the flame has been kindled, it will spread without limit if and only if the right fuel is available to keep it burning.

I have been part of a ceremony in which a central candle is lit in darkness, and then those encircling this candle may light their own candles after praying for Holy Spirit's wisdom. The darkness gradually disappears. According to Jesus (John 3:5–8), Holy Spirit is like the wind because it is mysterious. One does not know where it comes from or where it is going. So it is with Holy Spirit; its presence forces things to happen through us. Just as the

---

[87] https://www.jw.org/en/bible-teachings/questions/what-is-the-holy-spirit/.
[88] https://en.wikipedia.org/wiki/Trinity.

wind may empower a sailboat, with the proper spiritual trim of our souls, we may travel to destinations we would never have been able to reach without the mysterious, invisible wind of the Spirit.

Some believe that Holy Spirit has emotions like a person, but that is an anthropocentric view of God that fails to understand that Holy Spirit is often found at the extremes of *our* emotions. Holy Spirit is there when joy abounds and when emotionally crippling grief seizes us. It is in the times of our grief and uncertainty that Holy Spirit cradles us through to comfort so that our suffering may subside. It is our gift when we ask for silly things (Luke 11:9–13).

One instance of Holy Spirit present during abounding joy was my experience at A Walk to Emmaus, a three-day retreat that involved only one gender. We men, against our typical reticence to speak of our deepest feelings and worries, are gradually pried open by words spoken to us by men guided by Holy Spirit. As the experience continues, men are seen to reveal themselves, hold each other as brothers, weep uncontrollably, and come through with joy that was never possible before Emmaus. As one participant explained it, "I came here as an ex-con, and I am leaving as a child of God." It is as children of God (Romans 8:15–16) that we listen to the message of Holy Spirit with joy.

Some Christians further assert that "the Holy Spirit has His own desires and will."[89] This suggests that Holy Spirit is in control of us and has a plan for our lives. That is misleading because it seems to assume that Holy Spirit somehow has a specific plan for our lives. This reflects the mistaken idea that God is omnipotent.

[89] Chan F. *Forgotten God*. (David C. Cook, Colorado Springs, CO, 2009), 73

The truth is that Holy Spirit may have no control over us if we choose by our free will to ignore its presence in us. I do not think I need give a list of tyrants who have and still impel followers to harm and kill children of God. We all have a blatantly evil side to us that Holy Spirit must overcome. To tyrants, Holy Spirit is nothing. The hearts of many putative Christians are filled with the "us and them" view of other children of God in the world. Is a child standing at our border a reviled illegal, or is that child a hungry, exhausted, frightened little person in need of agape? Holy Spirit does not acknowledge man-made borders between countries.

Even today, tyrants may emerge from the church. I was brokenhearted to read that the patriarch of the Russian Orthodox Church supported Putin's invasion of Ukraine as a "Holy War."[90] That war has cost the lives of tens of thousands of Ukrainians and elicited great suffering because of the loss of homeland and the widespread experience of painful injuries. I cannot imagine Jesus supporting a holy war against a country full of God's children. Apparently, the patriarch and Putin have long colluded to keep the Russian people in line with Putin's political agenda. The Roman Catholic pope had a quite different view of the invasion; he is calling for peace talks to end this senseless invasion.[91]

Holy Spirit is not rock-concert spirit. When I was young, Elvis Presley was all the rage especially for young women. I've

[90] https://news.yahoo.com/russian-orthodox-patriarch-kirills-support-072928201.html.

[91] https://www.politico.eu/article/ukraine-war-pope-francis-condemns-vladimir-putin/amp/.

seen many old, black-and-white movies taken at various of his concerts showing girls in a frenzy over his presence. There is a spirit impelling these girls to act in wild and adoring ways, but this has nothing to do with Holy Spirit. Likewise, rock-concert versions of Christian gatherings have nothing to do with Holy Spirit. Many years ago, when I took my young son to a charismatic church, before the service formally began, there was a rock-concert warm-up period in which church members stood, waved their arms feverishly, shouted out praises, and even danced in the aisles all to loud music. After about ten minutes of this show, my son asked, "Dad, when are they going to sit down and be quiet?" I told him I did not know. Finally, they did pipe down. The sermon involved asking the congregation for money so the minister could buy a better jet to travel about the world and spread his version of the gospel.

The only way that rock-concert Christianity can claim legitimacy is if it somehow impels participants to go out into the world carrying agape to those who suffer. In my opinion, it is in loving others that we praise God, and not in rock-concert behavior. Indeed, one must have a quiet heart to hear the Holy Spirit's voice speak of love for others.

Holy Spirit—The Fabric of Time and Place

This brings me to one of the most important aspects of Holy Spirit's power that has not been directly acknowledged by theologians as far as I know. Let me begin with the sheep and goats story told by Jesus in Matthew 25:31–46 in which he declared that people of gathered nations would be judged by how they treated the stranger, the thirsty, the hungry, the naked, the sick, or the imprisoned. Those who denied that such people existed and refused to help them (the goats) would be condemned to a life of eternal punishment, but those who were righteous (the sheep) and saw Jesus in the eyes of the suffering would enjoy eternal life.

I recall this story because it is at the crux of Christianity and because it is Holy Spirit that opens our eyes that we may see Jesus in those who are suffering around us. In our times, this may be the lonely stranger, the mentally ill, the terminally ill, the grieving parent, the beggar at the street corner, the flood victim, or the lost child. You name it. If you are not sensitive to those who are suffering, Holy Spirit is not in you and you are not an ambassador of God. I hate to admit that too often upon reflection I realize that I have failed to see and act on the suffering of others. I make excuses.

Holy Spirit spreads Christianity over time and place. If one looks back at the history of the church, there were times of deep trouble and times of unification and compromise. Somehow, through the ups and downs, Holy Spirit flowed through the true believers like a river of pure, fresh, often underground water. This was represented in Jesus's words when he told the Samaritan woman at the well that anyone who drank ordinary water such as that from the well would become thirsty again but those who drank of the water he gave would never thirst again. Indeed, this water would gush up to eternal life. After a little more conversation, the woman rushed away to bring her villagers to see the Messiah. Jesus was speaking to the woman of Holy Spirit, the water that never led to thirst. Holy Spirit is the fabric of truth that flowed over time through the church despite all the human flaws imposed on it. I see a gushing over of Holy Spirit as I look at the modern Methodist cross with its flame. Holy Spirit has survived the test of time—until now. I fear Christianity without Holy Spirit is gaining too much traction in some places.

As far as the geographical spread of Christianity, I'd like to report my experiences in Russia in the 1990s when I went there as part of NASA's Shuttle-Mir program. Our plan was to repeatedly fly the US Space Shuttle to the Russian space station Mir. My Russian colleagues with whom I was meeting in Moscow asked one day what I would like to see. I told them I'd like to visit a monastery. The next day, I was sandwiched into one Russian's tiny car, and we headed out of the tension of Moscow into the countryside about sixty kilometers. The Russians have a much higher tolerance for risk than I do, so the ride was shall we say exciting. Once we reached Sergiev Posad,[92] we were forced to wade through an open market in which scores of Russians were selling all sorts of souvenirs.

In the monastery, a young Russian man who spoke halting English greeted us. The religious service was much different from those I was used to. A priest engulfed in a fog of incense was chanting and pacing back and forth just past a low barrier that kept us back. I was told that this was the time to pray and linger as long as necessary.

Next, my American companions and I were led to a line of people that was moving slowly. As we approached the end, I saw that Russians were giving donations and kissing the Plexiglas

---

[92] Sergei Posad: https://en.wikipedia.org/wiki/Sergiyev_Posad

(apparently) container of St. Sergei, I presumed, although preservation since the fourteenth century seemed unlikely. I said as graciously as I could that I was not comfortable doing that, so my hosts permitted me to leave the line.

My next visit was to a soup kitchen, where the very poor were able to get a meal. Soon, a bowl of stuff that looked like hash was planted in front of me. I took one bite and discovered that it was nothing like hash. It was a preparation from barley. Despite the disagreeable taste, I ate it all.

As I visited the chapel with its icons and paintings, I sensed without hesitation that Holy Spirit was at work in this place. Russians of modest means were looking after those who suffered abject hunger. They were acknowledging Holy Spirit as it came through time from their ancestor, St. Sergei, survived Stalin's brutal purges, and reemerged openly during *perestroika* of the late 1980s. Spirit spreads through time and place indeed. And often in mysterious ways.

▪ Holy Spirit's Peace

Peace brought by Holy Spirit is not guaranteed. One of the fruits of Holy Spirit is supposed to be peace. Initially, one can accept the Spirit's gift of peace when asking Holy Spirit to guide life's reflections and actions. What are the important injustices of our time, and how might each be rectified? What are limited individual capabilities good for in the grand scheme of righting injustices? Where will one find spiritual sustenance when emotionally crushed by the forces of injustice? One must ask Holy Spirit for guidance and power, but sometimes, the answer may be to keep going even though one cannot see improvement.

In the fight for justice, look past yourself to those beat down by injustice. Be present with them, counsel them through their suffering. You'll discover that your suffering will be less, and you may find some peace. The point is that peace from Holy Spirit will not allow anyone to ignore suffering or injustice; that is not the brand of peace offered by Holy Spirit. If it is, it is not Holy Spirit.

What Does Holy Spirit Deliver through You?

The work of the day in Haiti, mostly moving sticky, clay dirt in decrepit wheelbarrows, had ended for the day, and each of us in turn wrestled with the huge water bag to get something akin to a shower. It was 2011, and a cholera epidemic had settled in soon after the devastating earthquake of that year. We were in the countryside outside Port-au-Prince, where water was drawn by hand by Haitian women from a community well hopefully deep enough to stop any cholera germs. Our team drank only commercially purified water we obtained from a trusted store.

Evening was approaching, and it was my job to deliver the devotional for the day. After an interesting dinner that lasted longer than expected, the time had come for me to deliver, but I had no idea what to offer, and it was nearly dark. I wanted to offer a lesson on Holy Spirit, but I had no coherent way to present one. I pulled out the small New Testament given to me in 1990 for Father's Day by my oldest son and my daughter. I had placed tabs on about a dozen places where Holy Spirit was characterized. I decided to read each of those passages hoping that my companions would get the message that Holy Spirit was and is the fabric of the New Testament.

That was not going to be easy as I soon found out. The print in that Bible was small, so I needed good light to read it. The only electricity we had was from a generator near the makeshift church. Furthermore, the only decent light was one bulb hanging only fifteen feet from the generator. *Trust*, I thought. *This will work.*

My companions gathered, and I pulled out my New Testament. I explained in a loud voice that we were about to take a noisy tour of Holy Spirit as reflected in the New Testament. I loudly read each of the passages I had marked. I saw in the eyes of my companions that my message was sinking in. At the end, I asked for any questions. There were none, but there were looks of amazement on their faces at the truth of Holy Spirit. After reading aloud, I too felt renewed indwelling by Holy Spirit. Sometimes, the truth of the gospel speaks without any further explanation. Below is a summary of what I shared with my friends that night.

Jesus was conceived by Holy Spirit (Matthew 1:18–19). The Spirit of God was present at Jesus's baptism (Matthew 4:16–17). To the Pharisees gathered about him, Jesus warned that anyone who spoke against the Holy Spirit would never be forgiven (Matthew 12:30–32). John the Baptist reported to those gathered for his water baptism that Jesus was on his way and would baptize them with Holy Spirit (Mark 1:7–8). Holy Spirit is the ultimate gift of God in answer to our self-serving prayers (Luke 11:9–13). The kingdom of God, Jesus warned Nicodemus, could not be entered except by being born again of Holy Spirit (John 3:5–8). Jesus in the presence of a crowd of people declared that he was the source of a stream of living water (Holy Spirit) that would flow from within him to be received later by all believers (John 7:37–39). Jesus told his disciples that he must leave, but in his stead, he would leave the Holy Spirit as their Counselor and source of truth (John 16:5–15). Peter explained to the crowd gathered to witness the "speaking in tongues" of Jesus's followers that Holy Spirit would be poured out on all people in the last days (Acts 2:14–18).

Paul explained in his letter to the Romans that in our times of weakness and confusion, Holy Spirit would guide our prayers as our agony gripped us and we sought God's will in our actions. In this way, God worked for the good of those who loved God (Romans 8:22–28). Paul enumerated the fruits of Holy Spirit in his letter to the Galatians, the first being love (*agape* in Greek; Galatians 5:22–23). Peter warned in his first letter that Jesus's followers should not be suffering insults because each was blessed by the Spirit of God. In his first letter, John wrote that God was Love and God was Holy Spirit living in us (1 John 4:4–18). In Jude, the author warned readers to be wary of those without the Spirit and are further told to "pray in the Holy Spirit" (Jude 17–21).

There is a parallel thread through the New Testament speaking to the power of Holy Spirit. The thread is this: Luke 4:14–19; Acts 1:7–8, 10:38; Romans 15:19; 1 Corinthians 2:4; Ephesians 3:16; 1 Timothy 1:5. In these passages, the reader learns that Holy Spirit gives the power to teach and witness.

I have experienced this power at U.M. Army camps. On the last day of camp, we are asked to say something in front of the group that moved us as we worked on dwellings of the poor during the week. Generally, I try to keep my mouth shut and listen to what the youth have experienced. Sometimes, I feel powerfully called to witness to Holy Spirit, so I go up front, and the words seem to flow out from me without my planning them. Once, somehow finding the words of Reinhold Niebuhr, I reminded the youth that they were the hope for a better future that we older adults must have. The injustices of this world are not overcome in one generation. May Holy Spirit be with them.

▓ Finding Holy Spirit—General Approach

Some time ago, a friend asked me over lunch how he could find Holy Spirit. I opined that one could not find Holy Spirit as if one were searching for a lost treasure. One must have a plan for experiencing Holy Spirit and sustain that plan with undaunted courage.

The first step is to spend time around people openly living the fruits of Holy Spirit and especially agape love. Observe those people who project Holy Spirit from their hearts to love on others. Acknowledge the power you observe in these people and ask them how they maintain their lives in the counsel of Holy Spirit. Ask them to pray with you to experience Holy Spirit.

One day, you will know that Holy Spirit has become your master. You will be born again just as Jesus taught Nicodemus that one must be born again to experience the kingdom of God (John 3:1–12). There will be times of backsliding as one lives out days in a world full of temptations, but Holy Spirit will return to impel you to repent of your sins and continue as an ambassador of the kingdom of God. One day, you will be praying with others that they may experience the indwelling of Holy Spirit.

▓ Finding Holy Spirit—A Stepwise Process

Based on experiences of devout Christians with whom I have discussed this topic, there is a four-step process. In general, I do not like stepwise thinking, but I find that this might be helpful to those who truly seek Holy Spirit in a chaotic world.

The First Step

In all of us are the seeds of altruism but also seeds of selfism. Based on studies of identical and nonidentical twins, it appears that there is a genetic component to the balance between altruism and selfism.[93]

When we are young, our parents and environment determine which of the seeds will remain dominant and which will rot and die from neglect. When children see their parents doing kind acts, the seed of altruism is nurtured. When they are mistreated and see their parents mistreat others, the seeds of selfism prevail as the seeds of altruism rot.

The best way parents can nurture the seeds of altruism is by participating in a legitimate Christian community where kindnesses to all others including those living outside the church community are openly shown. Counterfeit Christianity such as

---

[93] https://sciencenordic.com/biology-body-denmark/study-altruism-is-in-our-genes/1421655.

the prosperity gospel or the idea of racial supremacy nurtures selfism to the detriment of altruism. Without the first step of nurturing altruistic seeds in the human heart, there is little chance of finding Holy Spirit. People in whom the seeds of altruism have rotted have no chance of walking the trail to Holy Spirit.

The Second Step

Second, we are to cast aside worldly threads that trap us in physical and emotional reality. This might be viewed as tearing away the spiderweb of worldly entanglements and thereby germinating the seeds of altruism. It may be accomplished in several ways. One way may be to speak in tongues as is common in many Christian traditions. The nonsense mutterings of a person may gradually detach her from the chaotic world that surrounds her. In the end, she has opened the door to the presence of Holy Spirit. This may cause a collapse into prayer from which she receives messages from Holy Spirit. Many people, including me, seem unable to speak in tongues. How do we find Holy Spirit?

Another second step may be taken through wrenching grief such as I experienced before my time of Holy Spirit capture (see the prologue). Grieving the loss of a child may be so powerful that all other worldly things are cast aside for a time and the grieving person finds that a door is open to Holy Spirit as the seed of altruism germinates in his or her heart. I remember feeling that I had passed before a door that could be approached only when there was nothing else left of myself. One is alive, but self is gone.

Another second step to finding Holy Spirit is by realizing that something is consuming the goodness in your life and must be purged. This approach is described early in this chapter by the woman who gave up alcohol cold turkey. It also seems to fit John Newton, the former slave trader who wrote "Amazing Grace." He could have entitled his song "Amazing Holy Spirit."

It seems that he needed two experiences to seal his relationship with Holy Spirit. The first happened aboard the ship *Greyhound* during a violent storm that threatened to sink the ship. He survived after laboring to keep seawater from the endangered craft. He admitted to backsliding until a serious illness fell upon him. His relationship with grace (Holy Spirit) was sealed once he found a new spiritual freedom from which he never balked.[94] He became a dedicated abolitionist and eventually was ordained an Anglican preacher.

The second step may also happen during group experiences such as Emmaus gatherings. Put together with others seeking a renewal of their Christian faith, powerful forces emerge to impel participants to germinate altruism in their hearts and open the door to an encounter with Holy Spirit. The story captured in *The Cross and Switchblade*[95] chronicles the effect of spiritual leadership and individuals working together to build the power to resist evil forces in their lives. In our model, we would call this a rotting of the seeds of selfism and making room for the germination of seeds of altruism.

---

[94] https://www.learnreligions.com/biography-of-john-newton-author-of-amazing-grace-4843896.

[95] David Wilkerson, *The Cross and the Switchblade* (New York: Jove Books, 1977).

The Third Step

We should accept the power and counsel of Holy Spirit once we have given away worldliness. Using our model, the seeds of selfism must be dead or nearly so. By accepting Holy Spirit as the basis of our spirit, we have entered the spiritual kingdom of God on earth and the seeds of altruism have become lovely plants for all to see.

As Jesus revealed, his kingdom was not of the world. He further understood that his disciples were to remain in the world but not be of the world (John 17:13–16). By his ministry, Jesus nurtured their seeds of altruism, and at Pentecost, the hearts of the disciples were opened and led away from worldliness by speaking in tongues. Then the third step came before them. Accept Holy Spirit into one's heart as one's life guide. Worldly Jesus had departed leaving behind the Spirit of Jesus, Holy Spirit. They now had bags of seeds if you will that they could spread far and wide to all who would receive them and turn from worldliness. The role of the church is to nurture the seeds of altruism through truths from Holy Spirit.

The Fourth Step

Fourth, we are to turn the power and counsel of Holy Spirit into actions that we could never naturally do on our own: witness to strangers, help the struggling, feed the hungry, heal the sick, and deliver the firstfruits of Holy Spirit without exception—agape love. Fight seemingly hopeless battles against injustice stemming from selfism controlling people in whom the seed of altruism has died.

We are to do as the disciples did—Risk our lives to grow the kingdom of God. Then and only then will we have come into full relationship with Holy Spirit and God. God wills that we agape others, all others even those we dislike (Matthew 5:43–48).

Unfortunately, this four-step process may be interrupted at any point and the putative Christian may never come into full relationship with Holy Spirit. Many people will stop at the first step—attending church regularly and enjoying the companionship of others in the church. The second step, abandoning worldliness, is something with which we middle-class people struggle. Even if we give up worldliness, we are reluctant to go forth with the counsel and power of Holy Spirit to risk everything to agape others. We are reluctant to demonstrate and fight near-hopeless battles for justice.

How Mackenzie Found Holy Spirit

A few years ago, I read *The Shack* by William P. Young.[96] Sometime later, I used his characterization of Holy Spirit to teach men in my Bible study class about the nature of Holy Spirit. Young does a wonderful job of portraying Holy Spirit as something like a ghost there as an interactive spiritual image but not really a person. I could relate to the story because it is about how a man named Mack found comfort in the shack after the death of his daughter Missy.

He was heartbroken. In the shack, he met Holy Spirit as an Asian-looking woman whom he could not put into focus. She shimmered as she collected tears from Mack's cheeks with a soft brush and placed them in a crystal bottle. Later, he did ordinary tasks such as washing dirty dishes with Sarayu (Holy Spirit) as she

---

[96] William P. Young, *The Shack* (Los Angeles: Windblown Media, 2007).

sang a hauntingly beautiful song. Later, Young explains, "Sarayu is the Spirit of God who restores the union that was lost so long ago … the human can once more be fully indwelt by spiritual life, my life" (pp. 112–13). Later, Jesus explains to Mack that he wants to be the center of a mobile that represents Sarayu's values. That mobile moves with the wind—the dance of being. Sarayu immediately noted to Mack that she was the wind. Near the end of his book, Young paints a scene especially poignant for me.

> Sarayu reached within her clothing and withdrew her small, fragile bottle [of tears]. From it she poured out a few drops of the precious collection into her hand and began to carefully scatter Mack's tears onto the rich black soil under which Missy's body slept. The droplets fell like diamonds and rubies, and wherever they landed flowers instantly burst upwards and bloomed in the brilliant sun. (p. 233)

After reading this again, I need Sarayu's crystal bottle in which she collects tears. I have left many tears where my son's body lies. Although it was criticized by theologians using fossilized doctrine, I think Young's lovely book does more for Christian thinking than anything written since the letters in our New Testament.

Holy Spirit as a Religious Bridge

My knowledge of non-Christian, Abrahamic religions is painfully shallow, but I can at least attempt to identify traces of Holy Spirit in two of these. My reason for attempting this is to ultimately suggest that Holy Spirit free of religious pomp, dogma, doctrine, fossilized hatred, and self-righteousness may form a bridge between religions that cannot be built in any other way.

Let's begin with Judaism. I'll dive into a fascinating lecture given a few years ago by a woman rabbi who had written her dissertation on how the rabbis understood the term "The Holy Spirit," or *Ruah ha-Kodesh*.[97] In Hebrew, *ruah* means spirit and *kodesh* means holy. She points out that there are hundreds of references to Holy Spirit in rabbinic texts but that the writers never claim Holy Spirit as part of a triune God adhering instead to strict monotheism. She points out that from the beginning (Genesis) for both Jews and Christians *Ruah Elohim*, the Spirit or breath of God, hovered over the face of the water. Ruah is viewed as a divine force flowing from God to empower men and women to speak for God.

In tamer ways, Holy Spirit makes Jewish leaders better able to be pastoral caregivers. In contrast to the Christian tradition of assigning male gender to Holy Spirit, Ruah ha-Kodesh, which is gender neutral, was regarded in rabbinic writings as feminine. The indwelling of God in rabbinic writings was typically feminine. At times, Holy Spirit was understood to be crying out with sadness at the injustices of this world. There is a view of middle beings between God and man of which Ruah ha-Kodesh was one. Rabbi Danan declares near the end of her lecture,

The power of [Holy] Spirit, the intimate, immanent, and moving

---

[97] Rabbi Julie Hilton Danan (2010), https://www.beth-elsa.org/Worship/ Sermons/Guest_Speakers/Do_Jews_Believe_in_the_Holy_Spirit_01_15_10. Unfortunately, this site has been removed, but traces of her view of Holy Spirit in Judaism may be found at https://wellspringsofwisdom.com/wp-content/ uploads/2016/03/Julie-Danan-CV-March-2016.pdf, p. 4.

connection with God, is as integral to Judaism as it is to Christianity. Moreover, in Judaism, this Spirit has a feminine gender, reflecting ancient traditions about feminine Wisdom and the Divine Presence.

As a Christian, I am not about to give up the belief that Holy Spirit is part of a triune understanding of God. It is simply the facet of God that is most accessible to me and that I want to indwell me. Jesus made it clear that he was departing this earth and was leaving Holy Spirit to be available in his absence. As far as any gender is concerned, haggling over this is nonsense. God is genderless. However, I would point out that most of the fruits of Holy Spirit would be associated with women and especially sacrificial love (agape) and that modern Americans view women as much more compassionate than men (see figure chapter 3). I think that many modern Jews would accept the attributes ascribed to Holy Spirit in the New Testament if they did not have to buy into its maleness and being a facet of God. In the end, what matters is how we live our lives under divine guidance. I believe that Christianity and Judaism are close on this point. Perhaps there is a narrow but passable bridge between the two.

Let's move on to Islam. The Holy Spirit is explicitly mentioned in the Qur'an several times. Samples follow in the text box.[98] The problem with Holy Spirit as understood in Islam is that the angel Gabriel is understood to be Holy Spirit and the words further refer to a subtle body of some kind that can penetrate coarse bodies such as ours.[99] Words used in association with Holy Spirit include

---

[98] The Holy Spirit in Islam and Christianity. http://www.islamforchristians. com/holy-spirit-islam-christianity/.

[99] Message for Muslims, http://www.message4muslims.org.uk/apologetics/ the-holy-spirit/.

truth and *guidance*, and it is in some ways a support to Jesus and is somehow involved in Mary's impregnation. While there is a huge gulf over which to build a bridge that seeks to span Christianity to Islam, one may hope that such a bridge no matter how fragile might be constructed.

About bringing the Qur'an down by the Holy Spirit, we read in the Qur'an:

Say, [O Muhammad], "The Holy Spirit has brought it down from your Lord in truth to make firm those who believe and as guidance and good tidings to the Muslims." (An-Nahl 16:102)

About his support of prophets and messengers, we also read:

And We did certainly give Moses the Torah and followed up after him with messengers. And We gave Jesus, the son of Mary, clear proofs and supported him with the Holy Spirit. (Al-Baqarah 2:87)

About the Holy Spirit giving life from and with the permission of God, the Qur'an tells us that he played a role in Lady Mary's pregnancy with Jesus. In the Qur'an, we read:

And she took, in seclusion from them, a screen. Then We sent to her Our Spirit, and he represented himself to her as a well-proportioned man. She said, "Indeed, I seek refuge in the Most Merciful from you, [so leave me], if you should be fearing of Allah." He said, "I am only the messenger of your Lord to give you [news of] a pure boy." (Maryam 19:17-19)

My United Methodist Hymnal has what is called a Traditional Native American Prayer. I will repeat that prayer below as an example of what one might call the purest form of Holy Spirit. By that, I mean that there is no dogma, doctrine, sacrament, or physical religious structure associated with the American Indian belief. The title of the prayer is "Prayer to the Holy Spirit."

> O Great Spirit, whose breath gives life to the world, and whose voice is heard in the soft breeze: We need your strength and wisdom. Cause us to walk in beauty. Give us eyes to ever behold the red and purple sunset. Make us wise so that we may understand what you have taught us. Help us to learn the lessons you have hidden in every leaf and rock. Make us always ready to come to you with clean hands and steady eyes, so that when life fades, like the fading sunset, our spirits may come to you without shame. Amen.[100]

The reason I greatly value this prayer is that it suggests the connection between the beauty of the Creator's work through evolution and our ability through Holy Spirit to appreciate that beauty. Personally, I feel this Spirit often as I walk in my favorite woods or see wildflowers blooming along our bayous. God's garden, if you will, consistently looks better than those I tend. If the time of day is right, I follow the sunrise or sunset looking for that moment when maximum beauty has been achieved. This is quite different from the Christian view of Holy Spirit. However, the prayer also asks that we find relief from having dirty hands and shamed spirits, which is consistent with Holy Spirit's call to righteous behavior.

---

[100] https://www.greatplainsumc.org/unitedmethodistprayers.

Prayer. Mysterious, indwelling Holy Spirit, I implore you to give me exceptional wisdom, power, and compassion when those attributes fail to come from my personal being. Help me set aside my hubris that I may see suffering in others and respond with humble, sacrificial love. Help me to gently counsel others when they are troubled, yet to act with power and courage in the face of injustice. Make me fearless in times when I witness my reasoned beliefs. Amen

Reflection. Maybe I have missed the small voice that calls me to love others in ways that reach beyond my personal capacities. Is this my conscience? Have I been too busy with my personal agenda when a friend needed me to stop and listen to her suffering? Have I spoken unkind words in situations where words of kindness and forgiveness were needed? Have I failed to acknowledge patience and goodness in others when tensions are high, and the best way is unclear? Have I ignored raw injustices that harm too many?

CHAPTER 9

GOD IS AGAPE

▓ Consider Discarding Anthropogenic God

Man tends to create gods in his own image often with exaggerated powers and unpleasant dispositions. The Christian idea that God created us in his image (Genesis 1) is turned on its head by the reality that we humans have tended to create gods in our image or at least the images we want gods to assume.

In an excerpt from his book *And Man Created God: Is God a Human Invention?* Robert Banks shows that from ancient times, there was concern that humankind was creating gods in its image.[101] He writes that the ancient Jewish prophets asserted that all gods except theirs were anthropogenic in nature. The difficulty with this view is that it is not the whole story. The ancient Jews wanted their God (primarily Yahweh) to lead in battle against other warring tribes of their day; it is what men did in those times. Thus, when Jesus came along in the days of

---

[101] https://www.abc.net.au/religion/who-invented-the-idea-that-man-made-god/10101104.

Roman dominance of the Jews in Jerusalem, the Jews wanted a warrior Messiah. That is what they were looking for and did not receive.

Jesus was just the opposite of a warrior god. He came to deliver truth in the form of agape love. This is unconditional, sacrificial, selfless, and in-action love. *At last, humankind had a God that was anything but anthropogenic.* If anything, Jesus's Father was not what the Jews wanted, and they certainly did not want it delivered by a country bumpkin from Nazareth. In the view from the first letter of John that "God is Love," humankind has attained an understanding of God as the fabric of loving relationships based on the principle of agape love. This is not what we modern folks want to hear. Jesus basically said, "Deny yourself, pick up your cross, and follow me if you are to be worthy of me" (Matthew 10:38; Mark 8:34; Luke 9:23). That does not sound like something created by man to foster his own wishes in a deity. The version in Luke says that this must be done daily. By my reasoning, Jesus's Father, speaking through Jesus, told us that we must give up our earthly desires as Jesus did when his time on the cross approached (Matthew 26:39). We are to project God as Agape Love to all who suffer in this world. We are to do this difficult task repeatedly in conjunction with the power of Holy Spirit. In my opinion, we, being by nature self-centered human beings, would never create such a God. Father God calls us to do precisely what we never want to do—give up ourselves and our wills.

▉ God Is Love

The complete understanding of God as Love is expressed in 1 John 4. The English translation of the Greek word *agape* as love fails to communicate to the modern reader the deep meaning of agape as used by the writer of John. As I have mentioned earlier, agape is unconditional, selfless, sacrificial, and in-action love. A few months ago, I presented this idea to a men's Bible study. I asked them to score the life of Jesus on a 20-point scale (up to 5 points for each of the 4 agape attributes) reflecting the degree to which he embodied agape. Uniformly, the men came back with a score of 20 indicating Jesus's life was one of ultimate agape. For perspective, the men generally rated Paul in the range of 15–18 points on my scale. How do the four aspects of agape challenge us?

Unconditional love means that no judgment is made of the one receiving agape. I cannot judge you as lazy, evil, unclean, demented, or arrogant and still deliver agape. This falls back to the axiom, "Judge not and you will not be judged, condemn not, and you will not be condemned; forgive and you will be forgiven" (Luke 6:37 RSV). This is a serious problem for me when I try to be nonjudgmental.

One way I attempt to thwart judgmental thoughts is by imagining how I would be if I had been subject to the same life as those I am drawn to judge. What have they experienced that I cannot fathom? Were they abused as children? Are they subject to serious mental illnesses? Were they reared in a household that practiced hatred as a badge behind which to live? Are they addicted to drugs because of their weakness for addiction? Are they responsible for their own health issues? I find there are some specific attributes I find difficult not to judge. These include greed, emotional or physical harm to others (especially children), blindness to the suffering of others, bearing false witness, and seeing only the bad in all things. What does your list of judgmental factors include? Which should be marked off?

Selfless love means that the one projecting agape love to another has no reason to expect any reward including even a thank-you. I also struggle with this agape stipulation. I like to be recognized or rewarded for the work I do on several fronts. I am disappointed when I have worked hard to be kind and helpful to someone who would never consider thanking me. It is my sin of pride I suppose. The lack of expectations, in essence, selflessness, creates a vacuum that favors the one delivering agape. If I have no expectations of a reward, it becomes much easier to discern even a tiny reward. For example, I have seen the opinion that the thanks from homeless people may be no more than an eagerness to receive more of what one has already given them. When I give a patient-safety talk to retirees, for example, my expectation is that they will seek to be involved in the movement for safer care. That is my selfishness. In reality, the vast majority want to tell me about their awful experience with American health care; it's about *their* experience. So in the fragile vacuum of selflessness, I am rewarded by stories from folks with no impulse to fix the broken system. Only in the vacuum of selflessness can one experience such responses as rewards. Their stories matter.

Selfless love can have its own impact. For several years, I worked as a volunteer at the Harris County Youth Village where boys ages thirteen to seventeen were loosely confined because of criminal activity but not violent activity. I was challenged to discover bridges between me, a middle-class, old, white man, and boys who had had little nurturing, were Hispanic or black, and were a fifth of my age. The bridges I found included playing chess, discussing fast cars, pondering the opposite sex, and talking about what happens when released. One question they often asked me was how much I got paid for visiting them. They were shocked it seemed to hear that I accepted no pay for my visiting. Why would I visit a place they mostly loathed without some monetary reward? This made no sense to them, but I'd like to believe it gave them something to think about when they were released.

Sacrificial love is well supported in the gospels. In John 15:13 (NRSV), Jesus said, "No one has greater love than this, to lay down one's life for one's friends." Ultimately, Jesus did precisely that. These days, one must ask, "What am I willing to sacrifice so that I can deliver agape to another human being?" One aspect of sacrificial love is the willingness to take a risk that the love, sometimes delivered as confrontation, will be rebuffed.

Here, I think another story from the U.M. Army might illustrate my point. My work team had spent three hot and nearly shadeless days rebuilding an older woman's large porch on her trailer and constructing a wheelchair ramp that merged elegantly with the sidewalk that led to her parking pad. We received no thanks for this, but she did come to our Thursday night dinner for clients we had served. Most of my work team sat at the same table as she did, but I sat with another client. As I was told later, at one point, the woman noted that she did not like our team because there was a black boy on it. (He was at another table.) One of the girls on my team lit into her about this raw racism. As the story goes, the woman was humbled, and before the meal was over, she apologized for her beliefs. I was proud of the young woman who sacrificially confronted injustice without fear. She had taken a risk as a youth criticizing an adult. Love is not always kind.

Ordinary sacrificial love happens when one sets aside his planned activity to help someone, perhaps a very old person, in need. For example (I've not actually done this, but I know someone who has done the equivalent), I may be due at a picnic at noon, and I am bringing the cold watermelon, but on the way, I see a person with a flat tire stopped beside the road. It is hot. I do not like heat, and I do not want to get dirty. Nonetheless, I stop to change the flat tire and then offer to assist the person in getting the flat repaired. My time-bound agenda has been sacrificed. I may be annoyed that this old person was driving around on bald tires, but I must not be judgmental. I apologize to those at the picnic who must now eat the watermelon last. I am sweaty and dirty, but I do not care. Small sacrifice.

Many Christians practice another form of sacrificial love— visiting the sick in their homes or in hospitals. One may dislike the reality of a friend suffering, but she must get past that to bring God as Agape to a person in need of friendship.

Radical action is the final attribute of agape love. I want to make it clear that prayer is not an action, but it is often a necessary *prelude* to action. Suppose one has recognized a deep need in someone who is suffering from the loss of a loved one or from terminal cancer. Prayer in that case is one's appeal for the Holy Spirit to be your Counselor on how to love that person in his time of deepest need. Prayer in this scenario becomes the template to guide action. Prayers that simply pray for another who suffers with no personal action are hollow at best. These might mollify one's conscience, but they are not agape, and they are not the work of Holy Spirit

▌ Agape and Justice

Agape is not always a one-on-one action with Holy Spirit as the mediator. Often, those who have discovered one of the many injustices in the world attack that injustice. When my son died, my eyes were opened to the gross injustices of the American medical industry. By Holy Spirit, I was given the task of rectifying those injustices. I was warned by an official at the Institute of Medicine (now the National Academy of Medicine) that my ideas were good but that nothing was going to change because too much money was being made the way it was. I, along with a few hundred other Americans, are trying to stop the injustices of industrialized American health care. I view this as agape love for the coming generations. I like a quote from a patient-safety champion named Donald Berwick, MD, in 2004.

> The patients whose lives we save can never be known. Our contribution will be what did not happen to them. We will know that mothers and fathers are at graduations and weddings they would have missed, and that children will know grandparents they might never have known. Holidays will be taken, books

read, symphonies heard, and gardens tended that, without our work, would never have been.[102]

In 2015, I coedited the book *The Truth about Big Medicine— Righting the Wrongs for Better Health Care*.[103] The chapter writers included MDs, RNs, PhDs, and change leaders. People knowledgeable of specific injustices wrote about what was harming people and what must be done to fix the harmful system. To my knowledge, nothing in the book made a difference. I was reminded that we writers are up against an industry that spends hundreds of millions of dollars on buying Congress. Those of us in the patient safety movement must pick each other up occasionally because we are constantly beaten down by a system that refuses to change from a focus on profits to a focus on the needs of patients. I'm reminded of a Franciscan prayer.

> May God bless us with **discomfort** at easy answers, half-truths, and superficial relationships, so that we may live deep within our hearts.
>
> May God bless us with **anger** at injustice, oppression, and exploitation of people, so that we may work for justice, freedom, and peace.
>
> May God bless us with **tears** to shed for those who suffer from pain, rejection, hunger, and war, so that we may reach out our hands to comfort them and turn their pain into joy.

---

[102] Berwick DM. From a card distributed by the Institute for Healthcare Improvement.

[103] Cheryl Brown and John James, eds., *The Truth about Big Medicine* (New York: Rowman and Littlefield, 2015).

> And may God bless us with enough **foolishness** to
> believe that we can make a difference in this world,
> so that we can do what others claim cannot be done,
> to bring justice and kindness to all our children and
> the poor.[104]

Sometimes, one must be the fool when it comes to injustice. I have personally found that raw verbal attacks may come with seeking justice. I've been called vicious names by some in the health care industry who would deny that health care must be made safer.

Here is another person's story of seeking justice in our sometimes-harsh medical system.

> As a very young mother and new parent/childbirth
> educator (29 years old), I was ridiculed and talked
> down to by several doctors when they could corner me
> and berate me for explaining things to women that they
> "didn't need to know" or "just wouldn't understand"
> or for telling them that routine procedures of the time
> (1970s/80s) such as episiotomy were not necessary for
> all births or all women and actually had no evidence
> that they improved labor/birth outcomes, future
> uterine prolapse, etc. Ironically, I became a rabid
> research reader, of both my nursing journals as well as
> medical ones, or at least looking at the meta-analyses
> of topical data. I kept records of it in my office when I
> began working within hospital education departments
> and no longer for non-profit education organizations,
> which the medical community effectively put out

---

[104] https://aheartforjustice.com/2010/10/07/a-franciscan-blessing-may-god-bless-you-with-discomfort-anger-tears-and-foolishness/.

of business. I would invite doctors into my office to review and discuss what they took issue with.

I was now their age or even older and literally had no fear of discussion of these topics anymore—I knew my stuff. Nurses around me would snicker when the doctors would back away from me and make excuses about how they were too busy to come talk about the topics THEY brought up to me. Interestingly, many of the routines (circumcision among them, as well as routine IVs, Pitocin use, labor induction) started being examined and questioned due to the harm they occasionally or often caused (higher infection rates, more pain so more drugs used, etc.). The hospitals' Joint Commission and insurance companies certainly paid attention, even if the doctors didn't want to change their routines or practice. Over 30 years of teaching and caregiving, I saw good and bad changes.

Sometimes years after I taught someone or helped care for them and baby, I would hear from them—I know I made a difference, one by one. Not big, attention-getting changes. Maybe no lives saved. But definitely improved. I felt better about some of the insults I had to endure when people told me that they made different choices about birth and feeding their babies because of the education and enlightenment—as well as being taught how to have conversations with their doctors. It may be hard to work for justice and change, but it's even harder to "let go" and not expect thanks, and just hope like [Hades] you have made some small or big changes for peoples' lives.[105]

---

[105] This healthcare education story was given to me April 2, 2022 by a friend, Maribeth "Mimi" Smith with her permission to publish it.

▊ Team Agape

If we as individuals try to serve the cause of righting injustices, the other side of the coin is seen when groups serve the needs of individuals. Not long ago, I returned from a five-day mission trip orchestrated by U.M. Army in Bryan, Texas. Each day's temperature reached to at least 95 degrees. I was assigned a team (Green F) consisting of another adult (an eighteen-year-old woman), a strong but inexperienced young man, and two girls who were first timers. We served three clients.

The toughest project was building a large deck to enable a grandmother with an amputated leg to be able to get outside into her backyard to watch her grandkids play. Despite two eye injuries (one from cement dust that sent a girl to an urgent care facility) and a serious heat rash, we completed a ten-foot by fourteen-foot deck matched perfectly to the back door threshold so our mostly wheelchair-bound client could safely get outside. She said she would attend our client dinner, and she did along with her cousin. It was then that my team realized how much our efforts meant to this woman. She was visibly excited about our gift. My team had lived agape—unconditional, selfless, sacrificial, and in-action love. We had accomplished together what none of us alone could have done.

▊ Asking For and Accepting Agape

Our pride often prevents us from asking for or accepting agape when we need it. We think we can handle all life's adversities without help. That may often be true, but sooner or later, all of us are going to need agape love. An example of this often happens in my faith community when older folks who have lost their driver's licenses need to get to doctors' appointments. Although they may be reluctant to ask for a ride because it will inconvenience someone else who has no obligation to help, at least a few do ask. Soon, someone, and often a stranger, comes forward prepared to drive the person to the appointment. This kind of help meets the test of agape. It does not judge whether the person deserves the help, it sacrifices the time of the driver, it expects nothing in return, and obviously, it is in action. Sometimes, this help requires great patience as wait times can extend to hours. Drives to and from the medical center in Houston can be daunting.

Because I have lost a child, I believe that my agape calling is focused on helping others soon after they have lost children and then later as bitterness visits their souls. It is not easy for me to do this, but when I hear of people losing children, I honestly feel Holy Spirit calling me to approach them with agape regardless of whether they have asked. Generally, they know about the loss of my son, and so the parents are receptive to visits; they know I get it. I go mostly to listen, to hug, and to magnify the goodness of the lost child.

Some folks I know have remained bitter for decades after the loss of a child. I have no solutions for such deep-rooted bitterness. At times, the bitterness is aimed at the mistaken idea that omnipotent God could have prevented the death. God through Holy Spirit calls us to follow Jesus's example and respond to such a deep loss. If the loss was because of gun violence, then fight those who think assault weapons should be abundant. If the loss is due to opioid poisoning, then fight the drug industry that caused the epidemic. If the death is due to a vehicle accident, then fight for safer roads or vehicles. If the death is due to cancer caused by a filthy environment, then fight for environmental justice. Fight injustice. Do not wallow in bitterness.

Trinity?

In general, I am not a fan of religious doctrines. These tend to obscure one's freedom to think and arrive at conclusions different from those who were ignorant of science more than sixteen centuries ago. The Trinity is a product of the Council of Nicaea in 384 CE; however, after some struggles with what to do with this doctrine in this book (or just ignore it), I decided to show how I believe it applies to the understanding of God as Agape Love. I'm aware that there are scores of attempts to explain the Trinity, so I'll wade into the polluted water hoping that famished alligators therein will continue to attack opinions other than mine. My opinion about the Trinity is reasoned from New Testament teachings and what science knows today.

God the Creator

God made all that initially was by something related to the big bang and made it evolve physically and biologically so that some 13.8 billion years later, life on earth became capable of understanding that God created the universe. Evolution has given us a beautiful earth, majestic mountains, colorful flowers, and blue seas (originally free of plastic waste). Evolution and our curiosity have beckoned us to discover a beautiful universe—the Milky Way with its exotically shaped nebulae and the distant clusters of galaxies that man's scientific and engineering skills and especially the Hubble Space Telescope have revealed. I sense that it was an act of universal love that God, through evolution, entrusted us with this beautiful gift. Our Father has indeed been good to us. But there is a problem.

Jesus and Suffering

That problem is that many of us who enjoy this beautiful gift of earth and heavens suffer from disease, malnutrition, war, and injustice. This is where the Son comes into the Trinity. Read Matthew 25:31–46 to understand that we are to see Jesus in the suffering of others. Because we are capable of agape love, our eyes are open to the suffering of others. Jesus's actions were the supreme example of agape love. Our response to those who suffer should be identical to Jesus's response—Heal them, love them, and walk with them. These days, Jesus is physically gone, but there are plenty who suffer. The Son of the Trinity is to be seen in the eyes of those who suffer. In that sense, Jesus is easy to find in today's world.

Holy Spirit

Holy Spirit has formed the fabric of Christianity since the days of Jesus; though that fabric was torn to shreds in many times past, it was still there. Today, Holy Spirit impels us to agape love as the first fruit of the Spirit. Holy Spirit enables us to respond with Love to others once we begin to see the Son in their sufferings. The

Spirit impels us to love our neighbors and even those with whom we share no bonds of friendship. Holy Spirit magnifies our seed of altruism. It is that simple and that complicated.

Thus, the Trinity is God the Creator of our evolution into beings capable of sharing love of earth and its people; Jesus, our Redeemer, is the suffering Son whose modern presence in fleeting presence in human history identifies targets for our love; and Holy Spirit, as our Sustainer, is the power in our hearts that impels us to see and act with love to relieve the suffering of others.

▌ Christian Roads to Agape

The diversity of Christian beliefs amazes me, but given the variety of understandings of God reflected in the Old and New Testaments, perhaps that is to be expected. As a scientist by nature, I look for a few or one core principle that must be true. Can such a principle be found in Christianity? I think so. Regardless of doctrine, dogma, tradition, sacraments, misguided preaching, sin, grace, faith, and anthropogenic theology, all Christian roads must lead to agape love. Any process associated with Christianity that does not explicitly do this is counterfeit.

If my beliefs are all about what God can do for me, I have totally missed the point. If my beliefs are centered on rituals and appearing weekly in church, I have missed the point. If there is anyone I judge to be inferior to myself or undeserving of agape, I have missed the point. If I pray constantly and have not given agape, I am failing as a Christian. Agape is God's will and God projected to others by the light of Holy Spirit burning in us.

Prayer. Holy Spirit dwelling in me, bind my heart and mind to your will. Make me project agape to others. Open my eyes that I may discern the need for agape and make me radically generous to those suffering souls. Blunt my arrogance so that when I need agape, I can humbly accept the hand of God, whether it comes in the weathered and gnarled hand of an old one or the soft, unblemished hand of a small child. Open my senses to the way God's gift of earth's beauty is being ruined by worship at the idol of greed and short-term gains.   Amen

Reflection. This agape business has got me thinking that maybe I need to live my life differently. How can I have objections to God as Agape? After all, if those who suffer in this world are to be relieved of their hardships, shouldn't I have a hand in making their suffering less? All around me I see obscene monuments that mask the beauty of plant earth. Should I go along with the crowd that builds these or be willing to accept the taunts that come with being a tree hugger? I want the courage to be different for a worthy purpose and for justice.

CHAPTER 10

PRAYER AND A LIFE
OF REFLECTION

▌ Worldly Intercessory Prayer

This kind of prayer asks God to intervene on behalf of the one who is speaking the prayer in some sort of tangible way. Simple examples include praying for safe travel to some destination or praying for a safe week until some gathering of the faithful happens again. Obviously, these prayers are almost always "answered." Given our relative safety from all sorts of bad happenings in middle-class America, such prayers are a good bet. Try such prayers in a blizzard or combat zone and the outcome may not be as you specify to your god. God does not exercise direct control over any such worldly events unless one is willing to give up the idea of a just and righteous God.

If you expect God to favor you with worldly blessings, you have missed the point of the Gospels. Jesus prayed to his Father to be relieved from the cup of crucifixion, yet he was crucified, being given divine strength to endure his suffering on the cross

(Luke 28:41–43). Paul prayed three times to be relieved of the "thorn in his flesh," but he was not given this worldly blessing (2 Corinthians 12:7–8). There are stories of Jesus and later his followers performing worldly miracles, but many think that true miracles ended with the apostolic age. As I noted earlier, miracles of the Spirit are not uncommon; I cannot believe in miracles of the world. God does not provide worldly favors to a few. That would be unjust and unrighteous.

Most of us have heard the expression "There except for the grace of God go I." It tends to emerge when we witness terrible suffering in another human being. Perhaps someone is suffering from terminal cancer or has been plunged into homelessness by a job loss. This view is misleading because again it supposes that God has favored you over the suffering victim. Since God does not single you out for worldly favors, thanking God for something God never did seems like an insult to God. It also is a distraction from the understanding that God is Spirit—Holy Spirit seeking your response, not your opinion.

▌Spiritual Intercessory Prayer

The lovely child's prayer (box), which first appeared in *The Spectator* in 1711, was written by Joseph Addison without the rhyming scheme familiar to most of

> Now I lay me down to sleep
> I pray Thee Lord,
> my soul to keep
> If I should die before I wake
> I pray Thee Lord, my soul to take
> If I should live for other days
> I pray Thee Lord, to guide my ways
> Amen

us.[106] It reminds me, now that I am an adult, that I am to come to reasonable belief as if I were a child. This simple prayer makes three important assertions.

- My life is not guaranteed even for another day, but I wish my soul to be in heaven if it does end.
- God is not in the business of calling me home, which is tantamount to killing me.
- If I do live another day, I want guidance from God.

The latter is best accomplished by accepting Holy Spirit into one's heart. Notice what is absent. There is no appeal to God to provide more days of life, and there is no request to favor me in the coming days beyond giving me guidance to live faithfully.

The most pointed passage in the Bible supporting this view is Luke 11:9–13. There, the writer suggests that you may ask for worldly blessings. God will not give you anything nasty because of this. God instead will offer Holy Spirit to you. Spiritual, intercessory prayer seeks God's guidance in difficult situations. One prays that Holy Spirit will guide me to know how I might help someone who is suffering or how I might rid myself of sinful behavior. The ultimate request of Holy Spirit praying is always to ask that I discern how to project God as Love (Agape) to all others including those I mistrust, dislike, or count as strangers.

St. Mother Teresa offered thoughts on prayer noting that believing in prayer alone cannot bring change but that it creates in us the power to know it is *our* responsibility to change what

---

[106] https://en.wikipedia.org/wiki/Now_I_Lay_Me_Down_to_Sleep.

must be changed by our service to those who suffer. From *Where There Is Love There Is God*: "The fruit of silence is prayer; the fruit of prayer is faith; the fruit of faith is love; the fruit of love is service; the fruit of service is peace."[107] Please note her certainty about what prayer does.

Later in the same book, we see the intimacy between Holy Spirit and prayer: "Above all, ask the Holy Spirit to pray in you. Ask the Spirit to come in you to pray." It is the spiritual change in us caused by prayer that calls us to action. As I write this, our news is filled with tales of mass shootings. The first was in El Paso, Texas, and the second in Dayton, Ohio, only fourteen hours apart. Twenty people were killed in the first, and twice that number were injured. The second shooting killed nine people and injured dozens according to news accounts. Reflecting on Mother Teresa's thoughts on prayer, how should I pray: "Holy Spirit, I cry out to you in anguish for the gun violence that kills so many in my homeland. I seek guidance on what I must do knowing that your counsel and power will guide me into loving action. My heart and mind are open to your truth."

Worldly Prayers of Thanksgiving

Good Christians often pray in thankfulness to God for some worldly blessing they are experiencing. I cannot reasonably accept this form of prayer unless all others have the basis for the same thanksgiving. One example that is unreasonable to me is to thank God for a beautiful, cool morning when in fact others in

[107] The writings of Mother Teresa of Calcutta by the Mother Teresa Center.

the world are dying in floods, being cooked alive in sweltering heat, or hanging on for dear life in the grips of a hurricane. Has God singled out your specific location on earth for physical pleasantness? Certainly, at creation, God ordained evolution leading to a pale blue dot that would have natural hardships and natural beauty for its occupants. If fate by chance has delivered a pleasant day to you, just enjoy it, pick a place on earth where suffering from a natural disaster is happening, and do something about it. A charity with very high ratings that I like is Direct Relief.[108]

One thing I too often give thanks for is the food placed before me at mealtime. We teach our children from an early age to be thankful for food, but I believe such thankfulness is woefully misplaced. Am I to thank God for food when hundreds of millions are starving?[109] Again, has God favored me in some worldly way? If I know that someone has taken great care to prepare an especially good meal, I thank God for the goodness and kindness put into the preparation of the food. Note that goodness and kindness are fruits of Holy Spirit. I also ask that the food nourish me so I may have the worldly energy to serve those who suffer. This is a spiritual prayer of thanksgiving that almost anyone can speak when they are given food no matter how meager it may be. If I have prepared a meal, which is an unusual

[108] Direct Relief. Extreme Weather, https://www.directrelief.org/emergency/extreme-weather/?gclid=EAIaIQobChMIh7jqmpem4wIVioTICh2q4g4qEAAYASABEgJAufD_BwE.

[109] WHO. https://www.who.int/news-room/detail/11-09-2018-global-hunger-continues-to-rise---new-un-report-says.

happening, then I pray silently that no one suffers GI distress as the result of my kindness.

▍ Spiritual Prayers of Thanksgiving

Often, prayers of worldly thanksgiving can easily be replaced by prayers of spiritual thanksgiving. If we keep fruits of the Spirit in mind and heart, we will find it easy to be thankful in a spiritual way.

One of my favorite things is to hold a child in times when that child may be suffering from the absence of a parent or from a nasty illness. In such times, I thank God that I have learned to be patient and gentle in such situations. Likewise, during the days when my parents were suffering in the last weeks of their lives, I was determined with the Spirit in my heart to be especially kind and gentle with them. In faithfulness, I prayed with my mom. While I wished my parents did not have to suffer as the grim reaper stalked them, I am thankful for the Spirit that impelled me to project Love to them and tell them repeatedly that I loved them.

▍ Prayers and Songs of Worship

Too many prayers during formal worship are rote recitation of words or delivered by someone else, usually an ordained minister. I do not believe this is genuine worship. In my opinion, there should be a silent time in which those participating in a service are expected to pray from their hearts and minds and not simply listen to others' prayers.

Traditional hymns may be the basis of worship. Many of these are so dear to my heart that I usually cannot sing them without choking on the words. Hymns that move my soul include "Hymn of Promise," "Thy Word is a Lamp," "Here I am Lord," "Pass It On," "Are Ye Able," "This is My Song," "Spirit of the Living God," and "Amazing Grace." Singing such songs brings me to my spiritual knees and opens my heart to the calling of Holy Spirit.

Reflection as Prayer

I was recently introduced to the idea of reflective practice as it applies to those who work in the healing arts. The idea is that in any given encounter with a patient, there may be an opportunity to ponder that encounter and ask yourself how it might have been improved. The most memorable reflection I have read came in a book called *Why We Revolt* by Victor Montori, MD. He tells the story of a time when he was a young doctor in Peru looking after a unit with fifteen very ill patients. His resources to help patients were severely limited. One young patient he calls Amanda was especially ill. The sun was setting as he approached her and sat beside her as she struggled to sit up. He held her withered body in his arms.

> She was barely breathing. She was dying in my arms for lack of justice … Her eyes said something too, but tired, they closed. I closed my eyes too, I guess. I knew. I think she knew too, calmly. She was dying in

my arms. I am now holding her tight. My breathing following hers … Her eyes opened one last time. She is too young to stop. Too young to stop. I felt her go. Leave. Death. Not alone. Did she feel love?[110]

Perhaps our best prayers of reflection are those when we ask, "Did she feel love?"

Reflection may take a simpler form, but it can also lead to serious soul searching. Not long ago, an older woman brought some cobbler to Bible study class and gave out small pieces on paper plates to everyone. She was somewhat disabled, and I suspect that creating this cobbler had not been easy. I like many others did not eat my piece. At the end of class, she came by and retrieved the uneaten pieces. No more than a third had been eaten. On reflection and too late, I realized that I should have held onto my piece telling her that I'd take it home and eat it there. I was ashamed that I had shown her no appreciation for this small gift of kindness. My point is that reflection should get under your skin. If it doesn't, you are reflecting on the surface, not in the depths of who you are and what you are to become.

---

[110] Montori V. Why We Revolt. (The Patient Revolution, Rochester, Minnesota, USA, 2017) 95-96

Prayer. Holy Spirit, always reside in my heart. Help me, I pray to resist temptations. Impel me to do God's will on Earth with each encounter of a child of God. Direct me to love the beauty of creation, seeking to preserve its natural form and purity. Give me patience and wisdom that I may fight injustice with courage and persistence. Open my eyes to those who suffer, that I may hold them as one of your children. Great Spirit, be the bearer of love during our fellowship time and in our singing of sacred hymns. Make a place for me in the Kingdom of God. Amen

Reflection. In the times when my life is going well, may I make the time to reflect on what it is that brings me joy. Is it love? Is it fame? Is it fellowship? It is intellectual pursuit? How have I been a part of bringing joy to others? Or have I? When times are hard and I feel depressed and unworthy of this life, may I find solace in reflection on the causes. Does sadness and regret change the past? How can reflection guide my future? Have I seen the need in others who may be suffering more than me? Is my life too much about me and not others? Would my suffering be less if I were to reach out to those who suffer more than I do?

CHAPTER 11

RESPONSE THEOLOGY— A SUMMARY AND PARTING THOUGHTS

In chapter 1, I suggested a set of attributes that characterize a God worthy of worship and emulation. The positive attributes were championing righteousness, empathy, courage, power, justice, truth, and inclusivity. The negative attributes that such a God must not exhibit are fearmongering, wrath, unbridled anger, vengeance, murder, and arrogance.

Dispensing of worldly favors must play no part in God's actions. Favoritism is incompatible with a just God. Moreover, such a God must be accessible to all regardless of times of joy or grieving, wisdom or ignorance, wealth or poverty, or sin or righteousness. The only way such a God may provide all these worthy things is by being the Spirit of Agape Love dwelling in us. That Spirit and sin forgiveness are the greatest gifts of Jesus.

Holy Spirit forms our response to what life hands us. If we follow the deduction of the apostle John in 1 John 4, God is Love and Holy Spirit. And by love, we further understand that in

Greek, love means agape love—unconditional, selfless, sacrificial, and in-action love. That is nearly impossible without Holy Spirit present in your heart.

I pointed out that another great gift from God, evolution, has led our universe through 13.8 billion years of physical development to culminate in biological evolution in the most recent few billion years. At least this is our earth's story, and it is scientifically known and well understood. It is not some ancient story bound into the times of its writing; it is for all time. Biological evolution has resulted in human beings who can understand the image of God in them that was sought by God from the beginning of time (Genesis 1). We know that we are the product of the amazing process of evolution that God created, but we must ask, Are we humans the final product of evolution? My answer is no.

Let's apply a little reason. In an overall sense, biological evolution is the joining of small parts to create a more capable and larger part that will survive worldly changes and catastrophes. Each adult human represents a cooperative of about 37 trillion cells that for the most part work together to preserve the organism that sustains the life of each cell with some turnover of course.[111] Logic would suggest that the next step in evolution would be for the billions of people on earth to come together to cooperate in preserving it so that we all may prosper as its cellular inhabitants. What will make that happen? Nothing other than agape love from each human.

I have used reason to attack some of the pillars of orthodox

---

[111] https://www.smithsonianmag.com/smart-news/there-are-372-trillion-cells-in-your-body-4941473/.

Christianity to blow the clouds away from the top of the mountain where truth lies. Holy Spirit is the bearer of truth (John 14:15–17). Is the Bible the inerrant Word of God? Read it critically. It is the compilation of the thoughts and stories of men who decided that they were under some ill-defined, divine influence at the time. Such influence is subject to the norms of the times of the writers. Times changed. The understanding of God changed. In the days of the Old Testament, return to the Promised Land was the goal, but there was prophesy pointing to a new covenant. The goal in the New Testament was to define the new covenant as one of the righteous heart in each person exemplified by Jesus's example, awash in Love, and powered by his Spirit. The Bible is the story of how we came to ultimately understand that God is Love. We do not depend on the ancient understandings that predate Jesus any more than modern scientists depend on flat-earth understandings. We know better.

When I have challenged some of my church leaders about the inerrancy of the Bible, they reply that it is by faith that we hold the glaring inconsistencies in tension. That is troubling. If one wishes to be a true Christian, one should follow the teachings of Jesus the Christ. I cannot fathom how one can find truth in many of the stories of Yahweh's behavior in the Old Testament and believe also in God as represented by Jesus or his Father. Of course there is tension, but the decision is clear for those who would apply reason to resolve the tension. Try using Rev. Adam Hamilton's Christocentric colander to sift for truth.

I further asked in chapter 3 whether a righteous and just God would dictate the exclusion of women from church leadership. Of course not. Justice and righteousness are not served by excluding women and their compassion from church leadership. Any biblical passages that point to exclusion of women are time bound and irrelevant to the church today. I might observe that the two major Christian churches that exclude women from leadership—the Roman Catholic and the Southern Baptist—are the ones with the sexual misbehavior scandals reaching well into the leadership of these churches. One might speculate that if women were in top leadership, such disgusting behavior would have been rooted out rather than tolerated and hidden.

A fresh report (May 22, 2022) shows that sexual abuse by many employees and pastors in Southern Baptist churches was systematically concealed by leaders despite constant appeals for action from those who had been abused. This strategy was apparently to keep church liability risk to a minimum.[112]

In chapter 4, I applied reason to challenge the belief that God is omnipotent—able to manipulate worldly happenings according to God's mysterious will. Can the view that God is omnipotent be reconciled with a world full of inequities, injustice, unnecessary suffering, natural disasters, and evil? Of course not. I pointed out examples of people who have been seriously harmed by this belief. Why did God kill my wife, father, husband, son, or grandchild? God did not. God is Spirit delivering Holy Spirit to us as the gift that allows us to become fully God's child (1 John 3:9–10, 23–24). We are to take up the crosses life hands us and with the Spirit's power carry them as Jesus would. This is our response to

---

[112] https://www.msn.com/en-us/news/us/southern-baptist-leaders-covered-up-sex-abuse-lied-about-secret-database-report-says/ar-AAXALws.

what life hands us. Life is unfair, but God is always fair; God is Holy Spirit empowering us to radical love. Such power gives us the courage to stand against authorities that would destroy our free will.

In chapter 5, I considered whether it was reasonable to believe that God specifically created each of us. It is not reasonable. What is reasonable is to understand that through evolution, God gave us the means to procreate. How we use such capabilities to procreate is up to us and our free will. Some will procreate irresponsibility with no intention of properly rearing any child born to the choice. Others will destroy growing life in the womb to avert any responsibility of rearing a child. Some will be driven by their sexuality to rape and incest, behavior never intended by God that steals free will from another. Each of us was created by our biological parents, not by God. Remember, God's kingdom is not of this world, meaning it is not of implementing conception.

If we by reasoning determine that God is not in the business of delivering worldly favors or miracles, for what may we thank God? Spiritual miracles. As described in chapter 6, these are the result of dramatic changes in our hearts and souls that enable us to leave our worldly baggage behind. Such miracles happen when we follow the will of Holy Spirit that we deliver agape love to all souls we can. In this way, acts driven by the Spirit impact worldly events. Conversely, worldly events may drive us with the Spirit to do things that we would never attempt alone. The miracle is that we do this despite our self-centered, worldly nature. We become the answer to the prayers of others through evangelism and being God's hands and love in the face of suffering. We seek to be present with God's love when others suffer. We do not walk by those who suffer as the priest and Levite did before the Samaritan rendered agape to a suffering man. We take risks because to love is to risk.

In chapter 7, I asked how the fear of God poisoned the church. I made the point that the Old Testament is primarily about fearing God, and we are not talking about respect; it is fear. The ancient Hebrews were expected to fear God or be punished in worldly ways via plagues, drownings, or military losses. The apostle John told us that love drove out fear. We must not fear eternity in some imagined hell because we do not buy into all the church beliefs, nor should we be righteous with the assurance that we will enjoy an eternity of bliss in heaven. No one knows what the afterlife holds. Based on witnesses in the New Testament, I believe there is a heaven, but I think we have no clue what it may be like. We cannot use reason to deduce the nature of any afterlife. This is where faith abides and reason plays out.

In chapter 8, I asked how the power of Holy Spirit was manifested. Acts of radical agape response. I would like to give four examples of lives powered by Holy Spirit or equivalently the Spirit of Jesus. These are stories of men and women with Christian backgrounds as Methodists, Southern Baptists, Lutherans, or Roman Catholics.

In her book *Risking Everything*, Sarah Colson tells of going in 1976 with her minister husband and four children to the jungles of Bolivia to live there as the locals did. Their goal was to relieve the endogenous, abject poverty of their new neighbors. The family survived many sicknesses, harrowing journeys, bodily injuries, and fear. Through it all, she relied on her faith and the Spirit of Jesus, which teaches that it is better to die physically than spiritually. Although not explicitly pointing to Holy Spirit, she acknowledges the ministry of God's presence. She writes of what I would call a miracle of the Spirit in which the indigenous factions put aside their differences to work for the good of all.

After returning to the US, she cofounded Servants in Faith and Technology. This has become an international organization dedicated to providing sustainable technology to those who suffer from poverty and diseases.[113] I had the honor of meeting and working alongside her son Tom in Ecuador in 2017. Sarah recently reflected on her life work with the poor in her new book as follows: "I could hear Holy Spirit leading me to seek answers to the question, *Why are people poor?* And the answers I found shocked me."[114]

Dr. Martin Luther King Jr. attacked racial injustice by risking his life trekking around the American south at a time when blacks were supposed to accept their role as second-class people. Between 1955 and 1968, when he was assassinated, King led the civil rights movement in the south. He endured a house bombing, arrests, a stabbing, FBI snooping, and plenty of criticism from enemies.

Please reflect with me on King's thoughts on how we can love our enemies.[115] He made three points. First, we must forgive our

---

[113] https://sifat.org/.

[114] Sarah Corson, *Untangling the Web of Poverty* (Lineville, AL: SIFAT, 2019) 37

[115] Martin Luther King Jr., *The Strength to Love* (Minneapolis: Fortress Press, 2010), 42–46.

enemies, but we do not have to forget the harm they have done. Second, we must understand that there is at least some measure of goodness in each person; he opines that there is both evil and goodness in each of us. Third, we must love our enemies as the only pathway through which we may befriend them. He clarifies that love as Jesus expected us to have it for our enemies means agape, which is God operating in the human heart.

Dr. Albert Schweitzer was a hero of mine in the days when I was trying to discern what to do with my life. He lived from 1875 to 1965.[116] He was a German theologian, musician, philosopher, and physician.

When he was thirty, he abandoned a promising career in Germany to attend medical school and become a medical missionary to disadvantaged peoples in Africa. He felt called by Jesus to this form of evangelism (as opposed to marketing religion). He spent forty-two years in Africa gradually building a hospital complex that contained scores of buildings. During World War I, Schweitzer was held as a prisoner of war in France.

He is well known for his unwavering reverence for all life. By far, the most worn book I have is one that compiled Schweitzer's thoughts on many important topics.[117] This was a gift from my parents in the late 1960s. Here are few quotes.

> Only in spiritual unity with infinite Being can [a mystic] give meaning to his life and find strength to suffer and to act. (p. 223)

---

[116] https://www.newworldencyclopedia.org/entry/Albert_Schweitzer.

[117] Charles R. Joy, *Albert Schweitzer: An Anthology* (Boston: Beacon Press, 1965).

> Mystical knowledge does not deprecate faith but completes it. For those who through the Spirit have attained fullness of knowledge the whole panorama to its furthest ranges lies in clear daylight. (p. 224)

> Although they [mysticism and reason] refuse to recognize each other, the two belong to each other. (p. 225)

> There is always the danger that the mystic will experience the eternal as absolute impassivity and will consequently cease to regard the ethical existence as the highest manifestation of spirituality. (p. 235)

Mother Teresa (1910–1997), now St. Teresa of Calcutta, became a nun and eventually formed the Missionaries of Charity. Many of her best ideas center on the need for love in action. But she cautions, "Love has to be built on sacrifice, and we must be able to give until it hurts."[118] She speaks about God trusting us to look after those who suffer and delivering love to them as we recognize that we must see Jesus in each person.

For many decades in her life (the 1950s to the 1990s), Mother Teresa felt separated from God. He was absent it seemed to her. Her spiritual suffering was apparent in many of her letters, but outwardly, she was a cheerful person. David Scott offered an explanation for her prolonged dark night of the soul; he noted that Mother Teresa observed in one of her letters, "I did not know love could make one suffer so much … In my soul I feel just this terrible pain of loss, of God not wanting me,

---

[118] The writings of Mother Teresa of Calcutta by the Mother Teresa Center.

of God not being God, of God not really existing."[119] Since I experienced a dark night of my soul after my son died, I feel a little qualified to interpret what Mother Teresa may have been experiencing. I escaped my darkness of the soul after a few weeks by understanding God was present in the love others brought to me and my family as my son died and was buried. I think Mother Teresa may have been so inculcated with the orthodox belief that God is omnipotent and was therefore playing a direct hand in creating the endless stream of suffering poor in Calcutta. Where was God as she dealt with this endless stream of suffering humanity?

I do not propose a clear roadmap to finding Holy Spirit, but I think there are four milestones that may be recognized. The first is that we all have altruism in us unless that seed has been neglected or destroyed by our environment. The second happens when by some seminal experience such as deep grief or speaking in tongues we nurture altruism, discard worldliness, and open the door to Holy Spirit's indwelling. The third step unfolds as we begin to experience Holy Spirit as transforming our will to God's will. The final step is to act on the will of God by sharing God as Agape love to those who suffer.

Have we made God in our image? In chapter 9, I suggest that the tendency to do this is evident in the Bible. Men want power and control, so in the days of the Old Testament as Israel was becoming a nation, Yahweh was powerful militarily and delivered punishment often though not always as evil tribes occupying the Promised Land were defeated.

The New Testament understanding of God, which was envisioned in the Old Testament by prophets, turned this understanding on its head. God was about right relationships, hearts filled with agape love, and power delivered in the spiritual realm by Holy Spirit. We were suddenly supposed to love our enemies instead of pleading for Yahweh to smite our enemies.

In a sense, both views are anthropogenic; they reflect two sides of our collective natures. Must we continue to try to dominate other countries by war? Our future cannot lie in that direction. Maybe all we need to know is that God is the substance Agape that creates right relationships, sees suffering in the eyes of the downtrodden, and acts to rectify injustice on all levels. If that is who we are, we are one with God.

In my opinion, if the music, creeds, doctrine, activities, programs, and teachings of any church do not lead Christians to agape love under the power of Holy Spirit, that Christian church espouses cheap Christianity like Bonhoeffer's idea of cheap grace. Ministries that point to what God can do for me should be set aside. Praising God for worldly blessings and ignoring the abject suffering of billions of people is unreasonable. Our pale blue dot is God's creation gift to us through an evolving universe. To besmirch the air, water and soil of Mother Earth is to turn away from God and God's great gift.

For committed Christians, I offer the following synopsis of

response theology pointing to biblical passages or less often to science and reason.

1. For God to be worthy of worship and belief, God must be good all the time. God must favor no one (Romans 2:10).

2. A creative force we call God molded the universe with its laws of nature and capability of evolving from formless mass through physical and chemical changes to biological evolution. Continuing evolution resulted in us humans. This is science. We were created male and female in God's image (Genesis 1:27) as spiritual beings capable of being indwelled by Holy Spirit (Acts 4:31). God did not specifically create us physically; our biological parents did that by their free will.

3. We have free will to believe in Jesus (2 Corinthians 3:12–18), choosing good over evil in this world (James 1:25).

4. The Bible is a collection of diverse writings that describe man's attempt to understand God and culminates in the witness and sacrifice of Jesus and the subsequent evangelism of his disciples. The Bible is not inerrant. Christocentric interpretation is the only way to reach the fundamental conclusion that God is Love (1 John 4:8, 16). We do not have to personify God; instead, we may understand that to the extent we need to know God, God is the spiritual force that bonds humans in loving relationships.

5. We humans live in the physical world where many of our choices cause good or evil. We may be altruistic and

choose selfless concern for the well-being of all others, or we may be self-serving as part of our evil side.

6. Life in this world is filled with evil events including starvation, injustice, racism, and oppression. Our world also includes natural disasters that cause suffering such as pandemics, hurricanes, and earthquakes. Any god that is good all the time cannot be in control of worldly events. God is not omnipotent or sovereign.

7. God's kingdom is not of this world (John 18:36). It is of the spiritual world where Christians form worldly actions with power and counsel of Holy Spirit to deliver altruistic acts by *righteous responses* to worldly happenings. Holy Spirit is found when we cast aside all our worldly baggage; however, we are the bridge between the spiritual world of our hearts and minds and the physical world of our eyes, hands, and feet.

8. The sole purpose of our prayers is to seek the guidance of Holy Spirit that we may respond by doing God's will (Philippians 2:13), which is totally encompassed by loving our neighbor (Romans 13:9–10). Love in Greek is agape—unconditional, sacrificial, selfless, and in-action love. This is the difficult challenge we face.

9. Intercessory prayers work only in the spiritual realm because God does not act directly in the physical world at the behest of our prayers. This would mean that God is arbitrary and unjust, hence not good all the time. God acts through God's Holy Spirit (Luke 11:9–13) and through that process impels us to be God's presence in this world.

With that understanding, we can state with confidence, "God is good all the time."

10. We are God's hands and feet in this world projecting God as Agape Love to all others. We are to experience the Spirit of Jesus when we see Jesus in the eyes of those who suffer (Matthew 25:31–46) never turning our backs on them.

11. Excluding women from church leadership is unjust and arbitrary. This is contrary to God's will.

12. Use of fear of hell to impel humans to love God is not God's will. Love drives out fear (1 John 4:17–18).

13. Gifts and properties of Holy Spirit include spiritual baptism (Mark 1:8), gift from the Father (Luke 11:9–13), mysterious like the wind (John 3:8), flows from one to another like a stream of living water (John 7:37–39), counselor and guide to all truth (John 16:5-15), available to all people (Acts 2:14–18), intercedes according to God's will when we do not know what to pray (Romans 8:26–27), helps us endure suffering and resist insults (1 Peter 4:12–16), and guides our prayers and mercy giving (Jude vv. 20–22). It is with these understandings that we can respond boldly to what life hands us. We must do God's will.

14. Fruits of Holy Spirit include agape love, joy, peace, patience in long-suffering, kindness, faithfulness, goodness, gentleness, self-control, and destruction of our sinful nature (Galatians 5:22–26). We respond to what life hands us with these fruits.

For those atheist or agnostic readers who rejected the theistic view of God, I get it. I also reject that idea of God. But I will not side with the deists or with the process theologians. My reasoning leads me to believe that God as Holy Spirit is in our response to what life hands us; this is response theology, which I believe is a new way to understand Christianity. I'd ask you to try to think about Holy Spirit dwelling in you and delivering its fruits in all your human relationships. That should be your response to life whatever it may bring.

Love and be vulnerable. Try finding a faith community that understands that God is Agape Love and has many ways to deliver agape to those who suffer grief, extreme hardship, or oppression. Avoid the apocalyptic communities, the prosperity gospel communities, and the Bible bangers. You do not have to buy the orthodox package of Christian beliefs, but I will bet that when you join Christians in team agape, you will feel the grace of God come over you. And then you too may become a committed Christian heretic/mystic believing that God is in how we respond to the chaos life hands us and others. There can be no wrong in that, but there is great power and truth. It is response theology.

Prayer: God of Agape-Love, empower us through your Holy Spirit to be your hands and feet on this earth that your will may be done on earth as it is in heaven. Open our eyes that we see injustice and suffering and humbly ask, "What must we do to further the righteous Kingdom of God? How do we with Holy Spirit co-create that great kingdom?" Mitigate our worldly cares that we may open ourselves to experience the presence of Holy Spirit when we are suffering. Turn our actions to those who suffer more, that we may be drawn from selfishness to agape action. As our years pass and we grow old, and our last sunrise has adorned the sky, help us to know in our soul that we have lived a life committed to bringing the fruits of Holy Spirit to many other souls. Amen.

Reflection: In the past I have struggled with the typical understandings of God. I could never get my head around the idea that God controls everything that happens. God is unkind and inequitable if that is the case. I certainly do not understand what is wrong with women that they are excluded from church leadership. I have also felt that the many rituals of the church do nothing that matters to the outside world. I remember trying to read the bible and was confused by the ambiguity of the stories and the huge inconsistencies between the Old and New Testaments. I gave up trying to find truth in that book. I have experienced spirituality in my life, but I never thought it might have had a connection to God. I must rethink that, leading with my heart instead of my mind. I promise myself to spend time with committed Christians as they reach out to our world filled with suffering and injustice. I have felt disappointed at those Christians who seem to think that it matters when they pray for God to deliver some worldly thing. Where is the love in that?

CHAPTER 12

CREED OF THE COMMITTED CHRISTIAN

A divine force we call Father God created the physical laws of our universe.

God ordained the creation to evolve physically and more recently biologically.[120]

Our earth is one of billions of planets that evolved in the universe over time.[121]

In the fullness of time, evolution resulted in life capable of pondering the nature of God.[122]

---

[120] M. Dowd, *Thank God for Evolution*. (PLUME, Penguin Group, 2007) 24, 36-38

[121] The Milky Way alone is estimated to contain 300 million habitable planets, https://www.seti.org/press-release/how-many-habitable-planets-are-out-there.

[122] We were made male and female in the image of God (Genesis 1). This must be a spiritual image in which the goodness in the Creator was imprinted into humans. Note that that the writer of Genesis 1 knew that there was a progression in creation not greatly different from how scientists now understand evolution.

Humans, given free will, created more humans through the reproductive gifts of evolution.[123]

Their understanding of God culminated in truth when God's Spirit became incarnate as Jesus.[124]

Jesus bore the sins of man's misunderstanding of God's nature and died on a cross for truth.[125]

Jesus was the bearer of Holy Spirit given to sustain us after his departure from earth.[126]

Holy Spirit counsels and empowers us to implement God's will of love in the world.[127]

Holy Spirit opens our eyes to others' suffering and calls us to act as God's humble servants.[128]

Holy Spirit impels us to identify injustice and act decisively to overcome it.[129]

---

[123] Your biological parents created you. God did not create you. Evolution gave you the power to procreate.

[124] John 1:1–6, 10–14. 8:12–47.

[125] John 16:36–37. Note that the understanding of God in the Old Testament is woefully inconsistent with the character of Jesus. This is well recognized as the Christocentric view of the Bible. The terrible acts associated with Yahweh must have appalled God. Jesus corrected that understanding.

[126] John 20:21–23, 4:24. Essentially, Holy Spirit is the Spirit of Jesus.

[127] John 14:15–21; 1 Peter 4:12–16

[128] Matthew 25:31–46 especially 35–36.

[129] John 2:13–16. This is clearly illustrated in the Good Samaritan story. We must never walk on by someone who is suffering as the priest and Levite did.

As disciples, we are in the world but not of the world; God's kingdom is not of the world.[130]

We are committed to loving as Jesus loved. God is Agape Love being always good.[131]

May the Spirit sustain us always even in the dark nights of our soul.[132]

---

[130] John 17:13–19, 18:36. This is essential and enables us to understand why there is so much suffering in this world, yet we must believe God is always good. God is not omnipotent in the world. God is Spirit exerting worldly change only through Holy Spirit impelling us to do God's will.

[131] 1 John 4:7–18; Galatians 5:22.

[132] Holy Spirit is there in our times of unspeakable anguish. See Romans 8:22–29.

Printed in the United States
by Baker & Taylor Publisher Services